## PRAISE FOR THE BOOK

In a world of confusion and competition, this book provides a refreshing breakthrough in how to uncover the immense power we all have simply by being ourselves.

Amanda Rose – Strategic Connector #BossLady<br>
CEO – Business Women Media

*The Albino Chameleon* is like having a best friend, a mentor and a coach all wrapped up in one engaging and inspiring book. In her warm and personable writing style, Kirsty shares both insights from her many years as a successful career coach in the aviation industry and stories from her own life. The result is a fascinating yet practical guide on how to put not only your best foot forward, but your whole, unique and talented self.

Hedley Derenzie, author of the travel-romance memoirs,<br>
*Finding Paris* and *Meet Me in Milan.*

In *The Albino Chameleon*, Kirsty references that people have trouble defining their own "wonderfulness." While that is true, defining Kirsty's wonderfulness is easy. Her passion, enthusiasm, humor, tenacity and innate compassion equip her with an impressive artillery which she uses to arm and mobilize her loyal client base. These skills, gleaned from years of experience within the recruitment and training industry, give Kirsty the insight and wisdom which so many more academic and theory based self-help books lack. This book conflates who Kirsty is and what Kirsty does—and I couldn't recommend it more highly.

Margaux Nissen Gray – CEO – MNGMNT Publicity, New York City

This should be compulsory reading for anyone embarking on an interview for a new position. Kirsty has successfully captured the nuances that are so often overlooked in this process. It is both humorous and educational and made for a thoroughly enjoyable read.

Sue Muller – Director – Pharmacy Employment Solutions Pty Ltd T/A LocumCo – Industry Leading Pharmacy Recruitment Experts since 1987

*The Albino Chameleon* is refreshingly approachable, light in tone and attitude but not lightweight. Ferguson has a writing style that is warm and relatable, preferring to populate her pages with anecdotal examples and not weigh it down in dry, empty platitudes we've all read before. The unique metaphor of an albino chameleon—a chameleon unable to use colours to disguise his true self, and therefore forced to be authentic in his emotions and responses to life—is employed to explore and develop what she calls 'the story of you'. It is essentially a guide to conquering that often-paralysing first question posed by many an interviewer, the dreaded "Tell me about yourself."

Marnie Hirst, Senior Editor, Hirstywords

Kirsty Ferguson is the GO TO coach for aviation careers. Her knowledge of the industry, the secrets to landing that coveted aviation role and the need to be your "best self" is a must-read for those inside the industry seeking change and outside the industry trying to get in!

Christian "Boo" Boucousis – Publisher and High Performance Coach<br>*World of Aviation* & Afterburner Australia

# THE ALBINO CHAMELEON

The Things That Make You 'You'
Can Become Your **SUPER POWER!**

## Kirsty Anne Ferguson

AVIATION'S #1 GLOBAL INTERVIEW & CONFIDENCE COACH

Copyright © 2019 by Kirsty Anne Ferguson

All rights reserved. No part of this publication may be reproduced, distributed or transmitted in any form or by any means, without prior written permission.

UnPack Media
NSW, Australia

Kirsty Anne Ferguson asserts the moral right to be identified as the author of
*The Albino Chameleon – The Things That Make You 'You' Can Become Your Super Power!*

All rights reserved. No part of this publication may be reproduced, stored in a retrieval system or transmitted in any form or by any means, mechanical, electronic, photocopying, recording or otherwise, without the prior written permission of the author.

This book and any associated materials, suggestions and advice are intended to give general information only. The author expressly disclaims all liability or any person arising directly or indirectly from the use of, or for any errors or omissions in this book. The adoption and application of the information in this book is at the readers' discretion and is his or her sole responsibility.

National Library of Australia Cataloguing in Publication entry

 A catalogue record for this book is available from the National Library of Australia

The Albino Chameleon/Kirsty A. Ferguson. 1st ed.

ISBN: 978-0-6487201-0-2 (paperback)
ISBN: 978-0-6487201-1-9 (epub)

Edited by Marnie Hirst – Hirstywords.com.au, Jude Lancaster, David Everett, Jacinda Cottee
Cover by Design by Sophie White
Book layout and typesetting by Sophie White

Printed by Ingram Spark

Disclaimer: All care has been taken in the preparation of the information herein, but no responsibility can be accepted by the publisher or author for any damages resulting from the misinterpretation of this work. All contact details given in this book were current at the time of publication, but are subject to change.

For more information about the author:

Kirsty Anne Ferguson visit:
www.kirstyanneferguson.com

Orders for this publication visit: www.thealbinochameleon.com
or www.kirstyanneferguson.com

*Kirsty Anne Ferguson*

CAREER MENTOR

AVIATION AUTHOR

THOUGHT PONDERER

SOCIAL OBSERVER

& CAREER BLOGGER

WWW.KIRSTYANNEFERGUSON.COM

WWW.THEALBINOCHAMELEON.COM

For Mum
A rare combination
of frailty and fabulousness

# INTRODUCTION

**A humorous, inspiring excursion into the question 'Tell me about yourself?'**

This book is an adventure, one that will uncover your unique story piece by fascinating piece. My profession is as an Aviation Interview Coach, however I've been called a 'personal publicist' a 'confidence cheer-squad' and the 'oracle of interviews'. My clients even refer to me as the 'O... of interviews' (referring to a certain megastar talk show host who we won't name). As coach to the top guns and airline pilots of the world, I've learnt a lot about what we share as human beings. How each of our stories differs yet contain elements that connect us. Your story, just like mine, is unique. It matters.

**Even if you think you have nothing special to offer, I insist that you do.**

My mission through *The Albino Chameleon*, is to help everyone say to the world **'this is me!'** and even look forward to the question 'Tell me about yourself?'

*"Normal is nothing more than a setting on the washing machine."*

Whoopi Goldberg

## CONTENTS

| | | |
|---|---|---|
| Introduction | | 9 |
| **1** | **Ben the Chameleon Fable** | **17** |
| | Chameleon Facts | 19 |
| | The Chameleon Conundrum | 20 |
| | *Building your story will unmask you* | 21 |
| | *The Albino Chameleon* is Born | 22 |
| **2** | **A Little Bit You, A Little Bit Me** | **25** |
| | The Future and You | 25 |
| | Rampant Self-Promotion | 29 |
| | I Was Only 16 | 32 |
| | Back Before the Noise | 36 |
| | What's on Your Innate Attributes List? | 38 |
| | Is All Motivation Good? | 39 |
| **3** | **Building Your Story** | **41** |
| | Choosing the Colours of Your Chameleon | 41 |
| | The Futility of Comparisons | 42 |
| | Get Going You—Exercise Your Chameleon | 47 |
| | Chameleons Do Not Roam Alone | 51 |
| | *Everything is About Relationships* | 51 |
| | Getting Control of Your First Impression | 52 |
| | *Relationship #1—Make Me Feel* | 52 |
| | The Dog Has Died | 59 |
| | *Relationship #2—Mentors* | 59 |
| | Lessons From the Bachelorette | 65 |
| | *Relationship #3—Shark-Infested Waters* | 65 |
| | Talking To Randoms | 70 |

|   | *Relationship #4—Short-Term Relationships* | 70 |
|---|---|---|
|   | On-Line Dating | 74 |
|   | *Relationship #5—The Soft Lens* | 74 |
|   | I Was Royally Called Out! | 77 |
|   | *Relationship #6—Surround Yourself With Honesty* | 77 |
| 4 | **What the Heck are Hacks?** | **85** |
|   | Helpful Hacks | 86 |
|   | Hack 1—Smash It Out | 88 |
|   | Hack 2—Forget About the Detailed Plan | 90 |
|   | Hack 3—Be Real | 96 |
|   | Hack 4—Neutering Nasty Stuff | 101 |
|   | Hack 5—Fall in Love With Failure | 105 |
|   | Hack 6—Be Cheeky | 110 |
|   | Hack 7—Mature Ego Versus Ego Maniac | 114 |
|   | Hack 8—Tenacity and Resilience are Your Best Friends | 118 |
| 5 | **Re-Write the Story of You at Work** | **121** |
|   | Career—What If I Just Have a Job? | 121 |
|   | *What am I going to do with it?* | 122 |
|   | *If you want change then change something, anything* | 124 |
|   | *Your job does not define you.* | 125 |
|   | My 'I'm Into' List | 128 |
|   | The Power of Writing It Down | 130 |
|   | What Moves Me to Act? | 132 |
|   | *Awesome Person #1* | 133 |
|   | *Awesome Person #2* | 136 |
|   | ReProgram Your Self-Beliefs | 139 |
|   | Do You Really Know How You are Perceived? | 142 |

|   |   |   |
|---|---|---|
|   | *Want to Find Out?* | 142 |
|   | Super Important Note | 147 |
|   | The Big Question—What Do Employers Want? | 152 |
|   | *My Capability Framework* | 153 |
| **6** | **Ready to Finish Your Story?** | **157** |
|   | *Here's What We've Got So Far* | 158 |
|   | This Is Me / Career-Brand Attributes | 160 |
|   | Become An Influencer | 165 |
|   | Blogging or Video Blogging (Vlogging) | 166 |
|   | *Take custody of your ogging!* | 169 |
|   | Deciding what to Blog/Vlog about? | 170 |
|   | Finding the Disrupter in You | 170 |
|   | *Change or fold. The time was now* | 173 |
| **7** | **I'm Not in Sales or Marketing** | **179** |
|   | What's In a Title? | 179 |
|   | What Is Marketing? | 181 |
|   | What Do You Have That the Market Wants? | 182 |
| **8** | **Chameleon Take-Aways** | **185** |
|   | Albino Chameleon Commandments | 187 |

| | |
|---|---|
| From Ben | 189 |
| A Gift From Ben to You | 191 |
| Glossary of Strange Terms | 193 |
| About the Author | 195 |
| Author Profile | 197 |

# CHAPTER

# 1

# Ben the Chameleon Fable

IN 1453, ON A SMALL ISLAND OFF MADAGASCAR, a panther chameleon named Ben was born to parents Steve and Jenny.

The Kingdom of Pardalis had never known an albino. Ben was albino. Almost transparent, apart from a pretty splash of green that would light up Ben's face when he was embarrassed ... which was often.

Large parts of the kingdom were incredulous that Ben could not hide his feelings. Something so natural to chameleons. It was difficult, even for the elders of the community, to decipher the thoughts or intentions of other chameleons since they could all emit their desired effect at will.

Ben was transparent in more ways than one. He had nowhere to hide. He could only be Ben. Despite this, he was popular. His even manner was reflected in his consistent colouring. He was considered thoughtful and pleasant, but most of all, honest.

He couldn't trick anyone even if he tried.

On one predictably sultry evening in late spring, horrible news spread throughout the Kingdom. King Furcifer had died in his sleep. For as much grief and chagrin this news brought to some, others were artfully plotting behind the veil of rocks and trees. Who, they whispered, would be the next leader of Pardalis?

Unlike most kingdoms, Pardalis was a democracy of sorts. The popular vote would elect the next king or queen, who would reign until death. As was the custom, the strongest candidates were paraded before the masses. They displayed their most attractive patterns and colours. Ben watched the proceedings with concern and of course, it showed.

"What's wrong Ben?" asked an elder.

"How do we know who is trustworthy?" Ben asked. "They all look like amazing candidates, but chameleons can display anything they choose, so how do we know which one wants the best for Pardalis?"

Other elders gathered around the conversation. Ben was politely speaking his mind, and his thoughts resonated with the wise, old chameleons.

More and more chameleons joined the huddle around Ben,

ignoring the grand posturing at the core of the important community gathering. The popular little chameleon had struck a nerve and before he knew it, Ben was swept up by the excited crowd and carried through the streets.

Ben's face glowed spectacularly.

The only chameleon unable to be anything other than himself, was now to be King. His 'flaw' had become his greatest asset.

Ben reigned over a blissfully happy Pardalis for many years. He never really got used to being addressed as King Benedict I, and his face would glow green…every time. And the crowd would laugh and cheer… every time!

*David Everett – Entrepreneur, Science Advocate, Surfer (my new hubby)*

## CHAMELEON FACTS

You may be thinking are Albino Chameleons real?

The answer is yes.

They are one of the top 10 most rare animals in the world, according to Google.

A chameleon is best known for its superlative camouflage powers. Its colour changing abilities allow it to blend in with any environment.

The Albino Chameleon however remains bright white regardless of his surroundings.

# THE CHAMELEON CONUNDRUM

People feel uncomfortable spouting their own wonderfulness and much of the time they don't know what makes them wonderful or unique in the first place. A big part of my role as a behavioural coach is to help people understand or define their attributes or in other words, their story.

I work with people from all walks of life, preparing them for everything they will face during the daunting process of getting a job.

The weird thing is they come to me with very similar issues. No matter which role they are applying for, it boils down to the same thing in a few different guises, the most common concerns centred around the questions:

*"What do I have to offer?" and "Tell me about yourself?"*

Every time you head off feet first into a new job or promotion interview, you have to deal with the gargantuan task of talking about you. Usually right at the outset with no chance to warm up or get a feel for the person you are facing across that desk.

What you have to offer is not purely about your career, and that is often where the confusion starts: what to include or exclude (and you haven't even started talking yet). We are much more than what we do for a job. This question comes into play in many aspects of life, like fronting up on a date or trying out for a sports team. Let's flip it. You are selecting a tradesman for a home repair, a real estate agent to sell your home or a babysitter. Now it is you conducting the interview, and I bet this question is up the front somewhere in one form or another.

The two things crucial to know about yourself as interviewee are: what do I want? And what do I have to offer? My premise is that knowing the latter will facilitate answering the former. I wonder how many of us have taken the time to define those things? If conducting the interview, you again need to know what you want and in turn, to find out what they have to offer. The thinking remains the same, no matter which side of the conversation you find yourself.

Just like Ben, in our day-to-day interactions we are attempting to be seen and understood. In order to do that we each have to build solid relationships, continue to grow and learn and attain a fairly good level of self-knowledge. The conundrum we face? **How do we both fit in with society and stand out**, at the very same time, all while being true to ourselves? To start to understand how we might do this I am going to pose questions. Questions that if acted upon, may well lead to a greater understanding of your own distinctive story and your offer. The ability to clearly and impactfully tell someone about yourself will be a by-product of building the story of you.

## Building your story will unmask you

*The Albino Chameleon* was born in an attempt to resolve this double dilemma, this confounding conundrum. By offering ideas, inspiring stories and the right questions, I hope to throw a little light on each of our stories as individuals. Shining that light on your talent, interests, attributes and motivations could lead, well, anywhere...

## *THE ALBINO CHAMELEON* IS BORN

I've always had something to say. I haven't always been sure of what I wanted to say, it's been more of a feeling that there was something inside me. Something I had to put out into this world of ours.

Still unsure, I decided to start and see where it led; to write and see what came out. As it turns out, I was compelled to write about the things that mattered most to my clients. Upon reflection I could see that those things also mattered to me.

It became apparent that everything I was writing seemed to apply universally. The issues I faced, we all face; the things I teach as a coach apply to everyone. The questions I was asking of myself applied to all of us, wherever we are and whatever stage of life we are in.

That's what can occur when you simply start.

At the beginning of any journey there is an intent, an objective of sorts, no matter how loose. As you progress, that meaning evolves and not always as you thought it might. It pushes and pulls you in a particular direction.

The trick? To listen and go in that direction.

So this book is me—listening to that direction and attempting to guide and inspire anyone I can to build their story or rewrite the story we all have.

**Defining that story can be the start of anything.**

**What if I have nothing new to offer, no story to tell?**

During my morning ritual of checking headlines or blogs on social media, scanning for those of interest and slotting them into my 'save' folder, I scroll past a myriad of offerings from coaches, mentors and celebrity gurus purporting answers to life's big questions. In some ways, as a communications coach I might be pigeonholed quite nicely as one of them. There is, however, one big difference.

Philosophically speaking, I relate far more to the label of 'disruptor'. Rather than a purveyor of answers, this is a role that contributes to change by posing questions.

Everyone's life and story is going to differ. It is my self-imposed challenge to ask the right questions to develop your story, as I already know you have one. Interspersed with a few appropriately borrowed witty quotations, analogies and stories of my own.

The first question I had to ask myself was:

**Has anyone done it quite this way? My way?**

My answer: **How can they? They are not me.**

A little bugbear of mine—I'm not a fan of solution headlines.

Headlines like 'How To Find Your Life's Purpose'; 'How To Make Your Passion Your Career'; 'How To Live Your Best Life'. As if anyone has the answers but you.

Let's agree to avoid those as much as we can.

If you do happen to fall into the category of not knowing what you are passionate about or even what you are good at, use the questions you will find throughout *The Albino Chameleon* to guide you, to help you figure it out.

I am not asking you to plan your entire life or any large portion of it ahead of time. Yes, everyone needs goals and a little direction, but let's not put that excessive amount of pressure on ourselves. The answers will come, just as long as we start.

No need to 'save the world' on my watch. Away with big life goals and micro-management style planning.

My ethos—just start!

Here goes...

CHAPTER

2

# A Little Bit You
# A Little Bit Me

## THE FUTURE AND YOU

NOBODY CAN PREDICT THE FUTURE, not that it prevents us from trying. Come on, haven't we all dabbled in horoscopes or had a sneaky psychic reading just for fun, even the guys? Well, maybe not. The future however depends on so many variations and coincidences, as well as pure unadulterated luck, it is impossible to know anything at all with any certainty.

Bear with me. What if 'predicting' is possibly the wrong word?

Instead, let's replace that with 'anticipate'. If we anticipate the future based on current trends and extrapolate those trends to thoughtful or even fanciful outcomes, we have a starting point. Or at the very least a red hot, trend-based guess at the future.

Let's apply that thinking to the 'Future You'. Right now, 'Social You' is no doubt positioned on one side, and 'Work You' on the other. They can be quite different; personality testing often highlights a distinction between your social and work personality traits.

If you haven't sat down and completed a personality profile test, I highly recommend it. Think Myers Briggs as the leading player in this testing (Google it).

## WILL YOU GIVE IT A GO?

WWW.MYERSBRIGGS.ORG

AND

WWW.THEMYERSBRIGGS.COM

OR

WWW.DISCPROFILE.COM

By the way it's not really a test, more a questionnaire, in case you find the thought of a test mildly off-putting. Many years ago I took one. It proved a light-bulb moment. It highlighted what motivated me, what drove me and why I gravitate towards certain things.

I found it eased what were the obvious confusions and contradictory parts of my personality. Once I discovered that most of us have four leading personality types rolled into one it helped me understand why I was a particular way in a variety of situations.

The future I see is one that involves each of us having our own brand. A great big mash-up of everything you are. Those things you are interested in, that move you, that frighten you. All of your life experiences in addition to your work persona bundled up and rolled into one.

Various parts of your life will make up the YOU brand. You can decide what those parts are.

Call it 'Your Story', 'Your Offer' or 'Your Brand'. Your resume will no longer be a dry old WORD document listing dates and jobs and qualifications, your resume will be all of you. From Instagram to Facebook, LinkedIn and Pinterest, the YOU brand will combine it all to create the Story of You.

That's how I see the trend in rampant self-promotion evolving. Evolving in a more constructive, purposeful way.

And it's happening now.

## RAMPANT SELF-PROMOTION

Let's talk about self-promotion. It has always been around but it is slightly different now. In this chapter, I'd like to touch on the arrival of a thing called 'rampant self-promotion'. Well, I call it that; I would even go so far as to call it a phenomenon. In day-to-day life we are inundated with YouTube clips, bikini clad Insta pics, food and even-more-food posts creating food envy en masse. Every second person is starring in a reality show and various forms of random, rampant, supposedly real self-promotion. Selfies made into books (you know who I'm talking about) and mind-blowing online business ideas proffered by 12-year-olds making gazillions. That is a hell of a lot of competition and it's worldwide! A frightening prospect at any stage of life.

In today's world, this trend may have the majority of its influence among the young or young at heart. That's where trends usually start, be it fashion, music or culture. It will not and has not stopped there. Business, authors, mums, motivators and exercise gurus. You name it, all have jumped on the rampant self-promotion train. It's how it is. It is... the FUTUUUUURRRRRE.

One of my influencers and fabulous self-promoters is Richard Branson, quite possibly because a lot of my career has been in the world of aviation. I recently attended a Success Conference in Sydney where Sir Richard was the keynote speaker. Now, did he just saunter on stage demurely and sit down for a pleasant chat? Indeed he did not! He walked in arm-in-arm with a bevy of Virgin Australia Cabin Crew, proceeding to cut the tie off the master of ceremonies; it's a Richard thing. Who else would do that!? Sir Richard had certainly arrived.

I suggest getting comfortable with self-promotion, it is here to stay and not just for the bold of ego. How you do this is where your control and creativity will play out.

## WILL YOU ARRIVE LIKE SIR RICHARD?

WWW.YOURNAMEGOESHERE.COM

Register your domain name before someone else does.

Open a LinkedIn Page and start connecting.

Start an Instagram Profile and post, post, post.

Make sure you learn about hashtags, they are important.

Build a branded Facebook page.
One you would be happy for people
who don't know you to read.

# I WAS ONLY 16

As we build your story, it might help to know something of me and where my story started. It all started with my mum. Mum was a rare combination of intellect and charisma, and I have dedicated this book to her perplexing contradictions. A teacher and opera singer who grew up after the Depression as the eldest of 8 (yes, 8) and was overlooked for a university placement in deference to her brothers.

As I left school at the end of 1981 (gasp!), along with thousands of other school leavers I was tasked with getting a job. At 16, I was a little younger than the norm, having moved ahead slightly at school due to our constant relocation from small town to small town. I was also severely undercooked. The physical presence of a 12-year-old and the street smarts of a chicken, compounded by zero work experience. A closeted private Catholic High School education meant I hadn't a hell of a lot of life experience going for me either.

I had several interviews on the horizon, some government, some customs and insurance, and some banking—every 16-year-old's dream! With no idea what I had to offer, what I wanted or what to wear, I turned to She Who Knew All. Mother.

Mother was purposeful. As I expand you might see why.

She appeared from the sewing room, a dress draped over her right arm. It was a shirt-dress in mostly white with a muted floral pinkish hemline.

"Put it on," she said. Ok, ok, I thought, not what I assumed I would wear to an interview.

I went along with it, and she promptly plopped me down in a chair. "Cross your legs," she said. I did. A giant split appeared up the side of my right leg exposing a good deal of my thigh. Shit.

"My mother's bloody well pimping me out!" I thought.

"You'll get noticed," she said. "Those legs are your only asset."

Right now, some of you are screaming "OMG that is so unprofessional, sexist and demeaning to women." Perhaps you are right. But by today's standards, that split was modest at best.

Did I get their attention?

Well, at the very least they remembered me for my attire, albeit not for that particular slip of the scissors.

And let's face it, she had a point. I had zero experience in any facet of life, even if her methods are now indefensible.

But never being one to shy away from the force that was Mother, I said, "Nope, you had best sew that up a bit Mum, I do not feel comfortable with that."

Now here's why the OMG'ers need to back it up a bit. My mother was a performer and as with every performer, she knew the power of the first impression, of grabbing the audience and making an entrance.

I'm sure that was all she was thinking in her attempt to launch me into some sort of employment (just until that right man came along – ha! – that's another story).

Did I get the job?

Actually, I was offered three out of the four.

As it panned out I was rather memorable, sans thigh high frock split.

Let me explain.

Mother had also given me money for lunch, a rare occasion and one to be savoured. I had three interviews in one day, no time to traipse home for lunch in between. I decided to grab something at the local cafe as a treat prior to my last two interrogations.

A meat pie. Mmmmm, a thoroughly Aussie/Kiwi thing to do. The meat pie arrived in a brown paper bag along with a small sachet of tomato sauce. The process is as follows: carefully, very, *very* carefully, squeeze the sauce onto the pie, then hoping it has cooled sufficiently not to burn the roof of your mouth, you bite into the top third protruding from the bag. No cutlery, that's just not how we do it, woman vs pie in paper bag.

I had not taken a single bite; I was in fact still depositing the sauce, at least attempting to. It was one of those squeeze packets, you gently squeeze both sides so it opens up in the middle in a sort of triangle shape, and oozes out.

This time, it didn't ooze out as it should... it spurted with wild abandon. I watched helplessly as in slow motion, a curved fountain of red spiralled into the air and... plopped onto my lovely whitish-pink shirt-dress, landing five centimetres above my right breast pocket.

"Don't touch it, you will only make it worse!!" my inner voice screamed.

Too late, I grabbed the nearest napkin and blotted.

Bad move, Kirsty, it was now a bright smear of red the size of a fist.

Disaster!

Worse still, it now looked as if I had stemmed the flow from a bleeding cut.

Yes, I went to the interviews, what else could I do? And yes, everyone mentioned it. Someone even offered me a jumper. Nice, but no: jumper over dress equals double fashion disaster.

Walking into the interview I kicked off by addressing the red elephant in the room, got it out of the way, also got a laugh. Thus it was a big red frock-blotch that made me memorable. In this case Mother was not wrong, just a little old school in her thinking around self-promotion.

What she also had failed to realise was that even at 16 I had things to offer. There were big bold indicators of who I was and what I could do, humour being one of them. The problem was, nobody had taken the time or had any inclination to point them out, to help me define them.

And I needed help.

If we cast our minds back, before all the noise of exams, of work and countless endless responsibilities, and think about those indicators, they will be there. Write them down, those are the things you inherently have. Don't worry if nothing comes immediately, that is just what we are about to figure out as *The Albino Chameleon* continues.

## BACK BEFORE THE NOISE

I'm going to walk the talk here. At 6.30 one morning, I did exactly that. Stripping away the noise of life, I sought out that simple 16-year-old still untouched by responsibility, regret or too many failures. I picked at my life day-to-day, grabbing hold of the ordinary things I had liked or done. Identifying those innate Albino Chameleon qualities. This is what I remembered. I was:

**The anti-kid** – anti everything. Yes, I was that annoying "But why?" kid. Until someone gave me rational, fact-based responses I would not get on board. Nowadays, you might call it playing devil's advocate. To this day, the ability to question, research and require evidence has been a big motivator behind achieving my goals.

**A non-team player** – individual pursuits were of more interest. I liked to do things differently, in my own time and not on anyone else's schedule. Today I know this attitude created self-motivation and self-reliance, whilst simultaneously infuriating my parents and teachers. Oh well!

**Not a great planner** – details didn't interest me, ideas and possibilities interested me, as did action. "Just get on with it," I remember thinking at school and in my first jobs. Details and planning are of course important and I now have colleagues that are particularly good at detail. One in particular would call me out during meetings and say "Look—Kirsty has seen something shiny on the floor!" In other words, she is off on another thought or idea. But I accept that is part of who I am. I don't mind being called out on it; well, most of the time.

**A writer** – I was and am a person whose thoughts are more organised when written. Albeit a shocking speller—isn't that what spell-check is for?

**An audible learner** – tell me something and I will grab hold of it. Be an interesting speaker and you have me. Reading dry text and facts… not so much. Entertain me with ideas and imagery and I am motivated. I see the irony, I am writing a book after all…

**A fast learner** – but unless I use it, I lose it. So yes, I was a last minute crammer. In my world today, that means I am motivated by deadlines. I do my best work three days out from an important deadline. I just get it done.

**Fascinated with History–** hopefully that means I am less destined to repeat it by having learned from what has gone before. Not always the case but reduces the odds somewhat.

**Miss Responsibility** – that made me a great employee, as I always tried to do the right thing.

**Bored by small talk—**cannot stand it, cut to the chase, get to the point. Talking about real nitty gritty, fascinating things is where I go. Perhaps a 'no' to a career in customer service then.

See? I told you they were there.

Kicking off The Story Of You starts by cutting through the noise and defining that which motivates and de-motivates. You will have the clarity and self-knowledge this thinking provides for life. Pick up a pen and commit it to paper.

Somehow that simple process, writing, makes it real.

## WHAT'S ON YOUR INNATE ATTRIBUTES LIST?

The Albino Chameleon could not hide from his attributes. He wore them on the outside; no matter how he tried, he was unable to mask them. Ultimately they became his strengths, his brand.

The Myers Briggs or DISC personality quiz programs are exciting tools that will unmask your innate abilities and attributes.

1. Take the quiz
2. Simplify the report by highlighting key or repetitive phrases or words. Create a list of 10 attributes based on the second point (you might even have two lists, one 'positive', one 'areas to improve')

But where does this list lead? It leads you closer to unveiling your story by deciphering what motivates and demotivates you.

# IS ALL MOTIVATION GOOD?

Whatever makes you start is good, I say.

So the answer is yes, even negative motivation works to propel us to act.

This may be quite obvious from the 'Back Before The Noise' thinking you just read. Some of which could be construed as negative attributes or negative-based motivations. That doesn't bother me, as even these facilitated action and so I have decided that no matter what, all motivation can work. Self-knowledge comes with all facets of one's personality, positive and negative.

Speaking of negative, as I alluded to before, my mother-daughter relationship was complex. A lifetime of polarising circumstances and her particular belief systems had resulted in periodic clashes of personality. Back then, my teen self had decided that my mother was the antithesis of everything I wanted to become at that time (don't worry, our future selves had a meeting of minds even if we were destined to never broadly agree). Her old school values and views on the world were more about what I couldn't do rather than what I could. Thus, I had found my first motivations in life and they were indeed based around the 'anti-motivations'.

In response to this a favourite catchphrase of mine emerged: "Don't tell me I can't!" You can imagine how that statement got me both ahead, as well as into a whole bunch of trouble.

I'll reiterate here that whatever drives you to go after 'it' is fine by me.

Plenty of time to sort out any lingering life issues. For now, propulsion, action and movement are key. It is this that will create change.

> *"A life spent making mistakes is not only more honourable but more useful than a life spent doing nothing."*
>
> George Bernard Shaw

CHAPTER

3

# Building Your Story

## You've Already Started

### CHOOSING THE COLOURS OF YOUR CHAMELEON

A STANDARD RUN OF THE MILL Chameleon uses camouflage to protect and disguise itself. Discarding that camouflage is difficult; it's confronting, even confusing, but very necessary in this 'building your story' voyage.

Taking an edit of those superfluous ideas, beliefs, and relationships still hanging about out of pure habit is challenging. Other people's opinions, beliefs and objectives will form part of that camouflage, they colour and influence our views and perceptions.

Once stripped away we have access to our original form, refreshing our thinking and objectives, realigning and redefining our chameleon colours.

> *"There is always someone taller, blonder,*
> *thinner, richer, funnier with*
> *decidedly better teeth. There is, however,*
> *nobody in the world just like you."*
>
> Kirsty Ferguson

## THE FUTILITY OF COMPARISONS

"There is always someone taller, blonder etc..." is clearly a quote for the girls, a version of which could apply to anyone.

It's a quote I use regularly when coaching to illustrate the futility of comparisons. Comparisons eat away at confidence and exacerbate self-judgement.

> *"Why judge yourself when the rest of the world*
> *is more than happy to do that for you?"*
>
> Anonymous

I prefer instead to be my biggest ally. Using my differences like little bits of armour I carry around as reinforcement. They remind me not to care too much about the distraction of others. After all, who wants to be a normal everyday chameleon?

The angst and energy wasted by attempting to be the same, having to be the very best or needing to fit in can be redirected to more purposeful and personal aspirations.

Taking solace in the knowledge that while I may not be the absolute best at any one thing, I am very accomplished at a wide variety of things. This is called being a 'generalist'.

Is being the best better? Does it make for a happier life or make one more capable?

Reality shows us that the opportunity to be the expert or the highest achiever in any field is limited. If that is the only value we place upon ourselves or others, our world would lack diversity, we would overlook the contributions of those who think or act differently. Rather than striving to be the best under a benchmark that others have set, I prefer to commit to the things I want to do, irrespective of the thinking of the day. To put my own unique spin on them. So far that has served to create the same or similar sense of achievement.

When starting my business, I was often reminded to "Keep your friends close and your enemies closer." I took that to mean, "Know your competition and watch them like a hawk." Compare, analyse and stalk them in order to stay ahead of them.

I did that for a while as it appeared to be a common business tactic, however I quickly realised they were watching me! Not surprisingly, they were doing a lot of the same things I was doing and therefore creating a circle of sameness. Sometimes I felt as if I was reading my own copy, just on a different website.

That made me angry—angry and frustrated. How dare they!

I would rail around the office, asking, "Don't they have a unique thought in their heads?" Going on and on, winding myself up and I am pretty sure, aggravating anyone within ear shot.

I was creating my own cycle and not a very effective one. So I stopped. Against the business norm, against my mentor's advice, I stopped watching them all together.

Gradually that shut out the noise of my competitors, and it was a relief.

I asked my team to monitor the key plagiarizer (ok, maybe a little latent resentment floating about) and only tell me what they considered would be of interest to me... eventually my colleagues also ceased that practice. We were not learning anything from 'Plagy' and all it achieved was a distraction from our genuine focus and mission.

There are downsides to accepting the unlikelihood of being the expert at anything. We must then accept the unlikelihood of being the first to do anything. Most things have been done before. It's more important to decide what you are going to do with what you have, and to do it with your individual style.

From a purely observational standpoint comparisons seem to create a sameness. "Ooh, that's what they are doing, it must be 'on trend' so I should be doing it." Trendsetters however do precisely the opposite. Trendsetters do things in their own way, on their schedule, with their vision, against the norm. They lead, irrespective of the standards of the day.

Often they appear immune to the criticism they are bombarded with on social media, the bullying at all levels of school and the glass ceiling or discrimination in the workplace. On the other hand, I am just as sure they are not. As I did, they stopped looking at their competition. They stopped looking at the negative comments, the trolls, the criticism and the plagiarizers. They stopped worrying about their level of education, their unusual look or lack of experience. A newfound sense of confidence and direction replaced the suspicion and distraction the practice of comparison evoked.

'Block' is a social media function I consider a friend. Use it liberally in your edit process.

## THE COMPARISON EDIT

Creating clarity around your chameleon colours.

Who do you follow, like, or associate with
that does not lift you up, listen, inspire,
make you happy or support you unconditionally?

**Find them, then block them.**

# GET GOING YOU
# EXERCISE YOUR CHAMELEON

*"It's never too late to be
what you might have been."*
George Eliot

George Eliot's eloquence—timeless.

As a coach I have been privileged to work with candidates starting a flying career later in life. Others were totally changing career direction to become business owners or university students for the first time, some at the age of 40. Then there are those with two degrees and ten years in management heading into the Defence Force or kicking off a career as a fire fighter, or wine maker.

I hold full admiration for each and every one. These people rock my world. They have courage, conviction and commitment. They are taking a risk, one that I don't know if I would take after 18+ years sequestered within my business.

Changing careers is not on my horizon, however I expose myself to new challenges frequently. Every now and again I too feel the need for a reality check, primarily to get one of those 'out of my comfort zone projects' done. The 'finishing thing', as many will attest to however, is not my forté.

You can't imagine the excuses I've rolled out. "I don't have time" is among the most common. But let's not suggest that I quietly put said project aside to come back to at a later stage. Oh no,

I can become quite dramatically overwhelmed, just ask my colleagues. The heavy sighs, the "I'm so tired", "I never get a break", "I need more help" and my go-to, "I can't talk about it—I'm not coping." To be brutally honest the project has probably hit a roadblock. It's become too difficult and I have lost clarity; either that or it's not going to plan. I've lost momentum or become distracted; typically these self-involved defeatist symptoms occur around 80% of the way through a project.

My saviour has been the realisation that I am not alone. These symptoms are part of the human condition, even commonplace, if perhaps less dramatic in some. Letting life's failures or hurdles become self-fulfilling is a demon I expel by referring to a simple pair of reality checks:

> It's never too late... and
> our failures do not define us.

That's how I know for sure that these people all had those same moments in some shape or shemozzle:

Age 23, Oprah was fired from her first reporting job.

Age 24, Stephen King was a janitor and living in a trailer.

Age 28, J.K. Rowling was a suicidal single parent on welfare.

Age 30, Harrison Ford was a carpenter.

Vera Wang failed to make the Olympic figure skating team, didn't become Vogue Editor-in-Chief, and designed her first dress at 40.

Alan Rickman gave up graphic design for acting at age 42.

Samuel L. Jackson got his first movie role at 46.

Morgan Freeman landed his first major movie role at 52.

Louise Hay launched publishing company Hay House at 62.

**So, get going you, your chameleon needs a walk!**

DO YOU USE AGE, TIME,
HEALTH OR EDUCATION
AS AN EXCUSE?

IF YOU STOPPED USING
THOSE EXCUSES, WHAT PROJECT
WOULD YOU START NEXT?

# CHAMELEONS DO NOT ROAM ALONE

## Everything is About Relationships

Yes it is.

The entirety of life is about relationships. About you relating to the dog, the boyfriend/girlfriend, the colleague, the guy in the street, the partner, the team member, the captain, the coach, the horse, the customer, the kids, the goldfish and on and on we go.

Most importantly, it's firstly about your relationship with yourself.

That made me think, so here comes the question (I told you I would be asking a lot of them):

**When we are communicating, how are we perceived and does that change from relationship to relationship?**

If we dissect your 'you-ness' in regard to relationships (that's a mouthful) or as a communicator, the story of you will continue to build.

Let's look at a few.

# GETTING CONTROL OF YOUR FIRST IMPRESSION

## Relationship #1—Make Me Feel

What's your first impression—of you?

Take a look in the mirror. Not at what you physically see, ignore that, but at what you say when you first meet someone.

Smile and introduce yourself—to you.

**What do you hear? What do you feel?**

Your relationship with yourself will underpin the impression you make when you meet someone for the first time, so it's important to get as close as you can to determining how you feel, when **you meet you.**

Every single time you meet someone it is the start of a relationship, even if you meet only once and for a short time.

Say you meet 20 people in one day, each of them just once. If you never come across those 20 people again, each individual will have left with an impression of you. Short and long-term relationships are both important to establish consistency around who you are in the world. Should we only put the effort into our long-term relationships or relationships we deem important? And, are we happy for those 20 random people to go away with an inconsistent or confused first impression? Here they all are, wandering around in the world with an "I'm not sure about her/him" opinion of their interaction with you. As we know, people love to share opinions.

I often wonder how celebrities cope, having to be 'on' all the time, being constantly judged for any suspected infraction or mood. Nobody can be perfect and graceful and caring and thoughtful all the time, I'm exhausted just at the thought of it.

How the hell does Queen Lizzy do it? Now in her 90s, she would have to be the most consistent woman in the universe. 65 years on the throne, waving and smiling and small-talking to the masses. Even if you don't agree with the Monarchy you have to say she does a stellar job. We won't mention the Lady D fiasco; bit of a glitch. Apart from that, pretty darn good.

My preference would be that everyone I come into contact with has a prevailing, consistent impression of me, the one I want him or her to have. Don't be confused, I am not saying that I need everyone to like me. I would like, however, to feel that I have presented myself in line with my personal and professional values and standards the majority of the time.

If they still do not like me, I am ok with that too.

That's still a feeling, and that's the aim—make people feel something and you tend to be remembered.

These days I find people will often confide in me, sometimes at the first meeting (go figure). "Why is that?" I ask myself. Possibly because I show an interest in them. Upon further reflection, I could see that I had made a few simple decisions a while back about how I wanted to be treated and in turn decided to treat others on those terms. Those decisions helped to develop a mostly consistent approach to meeting people. I say mostly as along with Queen Lizzy, I am imperfect and when in a mood can, and do, mess up.

The decisions look a bit like this: try to ask questions or give a compliment, maybe use their name a few times (if you can remember it, not always easy), also share some of your own experiences to find common ground.

It seems odd saying it, however appearing less than perfect helps others feel comfortable. It gets around any pretence rather quickly. I don't really have to work too hard on that one (chronic over-sharer alert).

How confronting is it to meet the perfect glamour-puss? Swinging her Chanel handbag and tripping along in her Jimmy Choo pumps? Here she comes, swanning into the room, everyone's eyes upon her as she elegantly strides across the threshold, until... she trips! Her perfectly coiffed first impression dashed as she lets loose a "F—k me", followed by a slightly embarrassed but genuine laugh.

You realise, "Hey, she is just like me, a complete muppet."

Irrespective of status, situation, success, failure, dress or differences, decide to see the best in people and hold back any judgement. Their thinly-veiled 'muppetness' will eventually reveal itself.

What have we covered so far? Be consistent, real, genuine,

imperfect, compliment often, and share—no judgement. Simply put, openness and honesty creates trust and in turn, an awesome first impression.

Now, some people have that warmth and honesty innately, but that's not the case with me. Back in the day the phrase "Ice Maiden" was bandied about frequently when my twin-like and clearly much younger sister and myself were on the dating scene. We didn't radiate that warm glow of acceptance and non-judgement at all. We stood in the corner of the Paddington Inn, sipping our pretentious pink Cosmopolitans and seemingly judging the hell out of everyone.

Only the inebriated or uber cocky would approach, we of course dispatched them at speed with a frosty retort or look.

If the aim was at the very least to socialise or meet people, how well do you think that worked? Ahh, not so much. Few got close enough to get even the slightest whiff of who we were. Own worst enemies comes to mind.

If we were expert at anything, it would be that icy detachment. Now held quietly in reserve as a piece of armour no longer required.

Back to my main point. Of the two questions I kicked off with, the second is the most important:

**What do you feel?**

How we make people feel at that first meeting will impress or depress.

On the social or dating scene my sister and I achieved exactly what we exuded, that if you come near us you will risk rejection, and we delivered that particular message effortlessly.

If a person is perceived in the following ways: "I don't get this person" or "I am unsure of this person" or "they seem to be holding back" or "it feels risky to approach them", then subsequently trust is not developed.

Genuine or frosty, interested or disinterested, shifty or open, the decision belongs to each of us.

We know that people like to spend time with others who they feel are genuine and will make them feel good. Seems a simple decision really.

Popping away the armour will feel risky. Without risk, as they say, there is no reward.

There are key decisions you could make to help achieve that genuine first impression. I'll list a few that helped me turn from Ice Maiden to Mentor and importantly to me, better friend and sister:

**Listen more than you talk,** nobody gels immediately with the great 'I am'.

**Ask questions,** it shows you are listening and interested.

**Devices are distractions and say "you are not important",** put them away.

**Be genuinely complimentary,** this starts any conversation on a positive.

**Acknowledge the point of view of others,** even if you disagree.

**Put your agenda away,** this is not about winning.

**It's not always about you,** share the limelight.

**Don't gossip,** it is a clear indication of someone you cannot trust.

**Be honest with your imperfections, mistakes and failures,** we all have them and everyone can relate to them, perceived perfection is daunting.

**Laugh at yourself,** you will be more fun to be around.

WHAT FEELING DO YOU
WANT PEOPLE TO HAVE
WHEN THEY MEET YOU?

## THE DOG HAS DIED

### Relationship #2—Mentors

The dog has died, was all I heard. I'm thousands of kilometres away in Perth, Western Australia and I've called my mum and dad to tell them something super important… I'm engaged.

Before those words had a chance to spill out, she says it… Dougal has died. He was with my father and fell down a cliff on Waiheke Island.

"Your dad is devastated" she said.

Dad loved that randy cocker spaniel. I start to cry uncontrollably. He was our family dog, our first dog; the naughtiest, cheekiest and yes, randiest pooch known to man. He had impregnated the entire neighbourhood back in our hometown of Napier, quite possibly the reason mum and dad had to leave! Little spaniel mixed-breed puppies probably lived on every street where a bitch resided.

"What the hell is going on?" I think to myself, sniffing back the flood of tears. I'm usually quite pragmatic about things. Who is this person?

Mum wasn't crying. She was straightforward about it. "Just thought you should know," she said.

The fact that I broke down in a serious flood should have been a sign. I was clearly quite raw and vulnerable. It was only later in life that I learned 'toughing it out' was my go-to survival technique.

Finally, sniffing back tears, I got it out.

"Mum, I need to tell you something, I'm engaged."

She didn't say much, just "Oh, I see."

"What does that mean?" I snapped.

"Well, it's just that you don't sound very excited."

"You just told me the damn dog has died, what do you expect?!" I retorted huffily.

"No," she said, "It's more than that you sound, I don't know... hesitant."

I *was* hesitant, something I had not yet admitted to myself.

"Well," I said, "I suppose I feel underwhelmed, really. I should feel over the moon, shouldn't I?"

"Yes, you should," she calmly offered.

"Why do you think that is?" I asked.

Mum knew not to rush in by providing unsolicited advice. It had not been well received in our previous, somewhat contentious mother-daughter relationship.

Then it just came out. I mean, I had no intention of telling my mother that I was feeling so incredibly vulnerable.

"I'm feeling pressured. I feel like he tries to control me and lots of other things and everything, really; um, I'm 24, I should be able to make this decision, shouldn't I?"

I was fumbling, searching for words to describe feelings I had until now been unable to admit. "Trapped, yeah I am feeling trapped like I was supposed to say yes and the next minute he had me out shopping for rings."

For the first time since I had left home at the tender age of 16, my mum gave me advice, simple matter of fact advice I have lived by and that I continue to trot out to my friends:

**"When you know, you know. If you don't know, then it's not right."** I left him that day.

*She, Mother, had provided a line in the sand, a rule that required action, it was exactly what I needed at the time. I needed to stop procrastinating and listen to my instincts.*

*When we go through experiences for the first time in life we don't have those guides, those rules, those lessons. We rely on the wisdom of others, others with more life experience to guide us, to inspire us, to mentor us. Having a mentor is having someone who does not judge, they instead provide a safe place to fall, be it that silly question you feel you should know the answer to or offering a different perspective.*

*I highly recommend collecting a bunch of mentors, suitable for the entire lifetime of new experiences you are sure to have.*

*Mind you, mentors are not infallible. Mother's past marvels of wisdom had ranged from the snooty, "Never be seen outside the house in track pants" to the spurious "Drinking sherry on antibiotics was discretionary." She never, ever failed to be entertaining... enough said.*

## Recognising a Mentor

No need to go off to a business group or wherever you think mentors spring from. They come from every walk of life, there is no formula. Consider someone you already know, anyone with qualities you admire and aspire to. Someone who makes you think laterally and challenges your perspective.

Mentors come in all shapes and sizes:

- School teachers or university lecturers
- Family members
- Women's or men's business groups
- Fitness trainers
- World leaders
- Entrepreneurs
- Community service organisations
- Sporting groups
- On-line forums
- People you follow on social media
- Business connections
- Colleagues or clients
- Friends and partners
- Authors
- Adventurers

Having a one-on-one mentor is not always practical. Some of my mentors are people I have never met, such as business leaders and bloggers. Others appear on open forums such as Ted Talks (www.ted.com) or podcasts, you can find one of my favourites 'Go All In', on Apple Podcasts. I can even say that one of my colleagues is a mentor.

Find them, listen to them, talk to them, learn from them.

### One of Mine

A lot has been written about Martin Luther King, not only because his words are poetic, but more so because he spoke with an understanding of the limitations of thought we place on ourselves and chose not to use them as excuses.

He had, for his time, an unparalleled grasp on the real issues of society. How we hold ourselves in the past knowingly or unknowingly. The courage it takes to break the thinking and bias of generations and the risks such change elicits.

He risked being unpopular, he risked much more than that in fact, but his risk has transcended the years, the trends, the issues of the day.

The things he was compelled to say are as relevant today as then and I choose to read something from him each week.

> *"You don't have to see the whole staircase,*
> *just take the first step."*
> Martin Luther King

WHO DO I ALREADY
KNOW THAT WOULD MAKE
A GREAT MENTOR?

WHICH FORUMS WILL
I JOIN THAT EXPOSE ME TO
MENTORS AND THOUGHT
LEADERS?

# LESSONS FROM THE BACHELORETTE

## Relationship #3—Shark-Infested Waters

Why do we make the relationship decisions we do? In any relationship, not just the romantic? An interesting question that science has addressed adequately, through the dissection of that thing called chemistry. Science helps us understand chemistry but it cannot, it appears, override chemistry and the way it seduces the intellect no matter how we analyse it.

How many times have you heard friends say, "It feels right, it feels safe, it feels exciting, we are just connected"? That feeling is the thing we crave and when it arrives, we recognise and like the familiarity of it. We tell ourselves it must be a good thing and we therefore keep recreating the situations that provide us with those endorphins. We keep repeating the decisions—whether good for us or not—as that seducer called 'chemistry' leads us by the nose and confuses our ability to intellectually decide.

I wonder is chemistry merely habit, simply a subconscious physical response to what we know? Is it therefore feeding and nurturing a habit, just like an addiction?

Deciding is something that our intellect does, perhaps at times to our detriment. It is, however, no competition for the manipulative qualities of chemistry.

I am reminded of the few enthralling parts of the Australian version of the "The Bachelorette" when in the final show she professes her love for one of two remaining contestants.

Not sure why I found myself watching. The TV was on and I had subconsciously seen so much of the promo material that I figured, ok let's see who she chooses. Don't judge me.

The overriding issue in this actress-come-songstress's life was she traditionally selected high profile, player types with the ego-maturity of a cumquat.

Her mission, should she choose to accept it, was to disregard her natural propensity to go for excitement, the risky dude, the flamboyant big shot and find someone normal. Someone she could rely on and build a family with. Someone who had her back no matter what. No issues, no drama, just a good solid bloke—in Aussie terms that's called 'a keeper'.

To do that, I thought, she had to be prepared to override that overrated physical response called chemistry.

Chemistry, we agree, will help you repeat the same mistakes or remake the same choices from the past. As we grow in experience most of us realise that chemistry doesn't always last and relationships take a lot of practical things to make them work.

Intellect however has a huge battle on its hands.

I put that aside and took the Bachelorette at her word, hoping against hope she could break her cycle. She was so damn genuine about it. It takes a huge commitment to your goals and an advanced level of self-awareness to stick to that decision, and it *is* a decision. Overcoming an addiction, and I am classing chemistry as one, will not be easy.

Then, you guessed it, she chose the player, the multi-millionaire, full of baggage, already-had-a-vasectomy man about town. "NOOOOOO," I cried, "don't do it!" I was devastated, I so wanted her to show all my 30-something friends it can be done. That the wholesome, genuine, caring, emotionally connected guy can be triumphant.

Sigh...but no, she didn't choose him.

She actually said something along these lines to the runner up, "You are everything my head told me I wanted, but I have fallen in love with someone else."

Phhhffft!

Ok, I'm not her and I always want people to be happy, so I hope they prove me wrong. Not holding my breath.

Glad I didn't (hold my breath that is). A few months later their love had faded and deflated like an old pool toy in the summer sun.

### The Take-Away

Until we are really ready to back ourselves 100%, to put ego in its place and conquer pure emotional responses we are never likely to rewrite the relationship script of our lives.

In order to kick off the rewrite and truly commit to what we want we must remind ourselves of our mistakes. Don't let them fade. If we ignore history we are destined to repeat it.

If we waiver in our commitment to ourselves and our goals, we are destined to circle for eternity in the same shark-infested waters.

## A Note to My Friends and Readers

There are two types of people in our lives, those who have got your back, and those who have got no idea.

I am not sure who said it first or where the research to back this up is, but I am going to regurgitate this statement with the confidence that unequivocally applies to my circle of friends:

> *"You are the sum of the five people you spend the most time with."*
> Unknown

When it comes to choosing the people in your life I advocate taking a very tough stance.

Friends, partners, acquaintances and colleagues, these are the pool of people you are selecting as part of your influencer team. They will help you be the very best version of you or encourage the worst.

Be rigorous in rooting out the latter, they will suck your energy, undermine your confidence and reinforce destructive behaviours.

> *"It's better to conquer oneself than to win a thousand battles."*
> Buddha

# WHICH RELATIONSHIPS DO YOU NEED TO REASSESS?

# TALKING TO RANDOMS

## Relationship #4—Short-Term Relationships

Short-term relationships occur every day, anywhere. Fleeting, heartfelt, unusual or even mundane, each has definable takeaways.

### The Check-Out Lady, the Opera Singer and The Widow

Sunday evening, 6pm, Coles Supermarket checkout: "I'm five years away from retirement, my husband retired last year however we can do with a little extra cash so here I am working at Coles. It's just two shifts a week, but it keeps the money coming in, and let's face it, now that he is home all the time, sigh, getting out of the house isn't a bad thing.

I've given him odd jobs to do around the house to keep him busy, but they don't seem to get done when I'm not there. I don't want to turn into a nag so I might pick up a few extra shifts here just to keep out of the way.

My son is a travel agent, you know. He's always away so we don't see him much, but that's ok, they have to live their own lives. No point hanging around here just because I miss him. You know what I mean?"

### Thursday Morning, 22 Grams Café

A 30-something gentleman sits with who I assume is his dad. We are in close proximity. I'm writing but easily distracted by the comings and goings. He breaks into a whispered song; I think I recognise a few bars. "Is that Puccini?" I ask, not embarrassed at all. He says in a typically booming operatic voice, "Yes it's from Tosca." His dad steps away, the conversation continues.

He is from Germany and in town to perform at a special Opera House event. "How did you know it was Puccini?" he enquires. "My mum was an opera singer. Mum trained in New Zealand with Dame Sister Mary Leo, who also trained Kiri Te Kanawa. I have been around classical music all my life." I quickly add "No, I don't sing," and he laughs.

### Saturday Morning, Dog Park

A young Schnauzer romps up to me. "Hello boy!" He jumps into play stance and Bentley (my dog) and he race off to play.

Schnauzer dog mum approaches, probably early 60s, very well spoken and I soon find out she is a local artist about to have an exhibition in the Blue Mountains.

There is something about her that makes me feel I should stay, that company is somehow important to her this morning. As the conversation progresses, I am privy to a very personal revelation.

She is about to drive to her holiday house to 'clean up'.

Her husband had been dying of cancer and he'd taken himself off to their holiday home for some peace and quiet. Without her knowledge, and in a place and time of his choosing, her husband had decided to euthanize himself.

In the hour that passed we chatted in spurts and sat quietly watching the dogs, who occasionally wandered over for a pat and to check on us, racing off as quickly as they had arrived.

Unable to postpone the progression of my day any longer, I found myself warmly embracing this petite, perfectly groomed stranger. I too knew the confusion of such confounding loss.

**The world is full of interesting stories, talk to everyone who wants to talk to you.**

WHICH COMPLETE
STRANGER HAVE YOU
TALKED TO THIS WEEK?

WHAT DID YOU OBSERVE
ABOUT YOURSELF?

# ON-LINE DATING

## Relationship #5—The Soft Lens

Slim or sporty?

That was the question that stumped me a few years ago when I tentatively stepped into what was, for me, the risky world of on-line dating. I was leaning towards sporty due to my active lifestyle and firm focus on health rather than weight.

My house mate said, "Ahhhhh, that would be slim, Kirsty".

She didn't seem confused about defining my body type at all.

"I see," I said. In a slightly huffy tone.

Was this a soft lens I had placed on my version of me, post-divorce and over 40? Just wait until I get my hands on your profile, I thought to myself, I was writing hers next.

On-line dating, I was to discover with the most reputable sites, requires a good deal of introspection as you wade through the personality profiling or as we coaches call it, psychometric testing.

It's not all "I love puppy dogs and walks on the beach." They match you through proper psychometric testing—who knew?

Anyway, I got through the testing questions, there were a lot and I was now on to the profile itself. This could attract or repel a good deal of contestants-I-mean-suitors (that's a bit old fashioned but what else do you call them? Mates? Dates? Hook-ups?). I suppose it would repel those who were totally unsuitable, not a bad thing. If I receive only a few responses, at least it will have stopped all the time wasters.

Justify, justify, justify—I was doing it already, just in case I didn't get many contacts.

Stop it Kirsty!

What to write? Come on girl, you are a writer, just start. That's what you tell everyone else.

Right, I'm going to treat it as a self-branding exercise, what defines me, be honest, be witty and be open. These were a few of the rules running around in my head.

First contact: "You follow Rugby League?"

That would be a no. No self-respecting Kiwi (New Zelander) could date anyone but a Rugby Union supporter. Hang on Kirsty, are you being judgemental? Yes, you are, he seems lovely. Just start a conversation. So I did—for 2 emails. League was a deal breaker.

Now please don't think I am being petty, I was learning how to sift through this stuff and be outrageously open with who I was. I had sucked up not being sporty and realised I was unapologetically prejudiced about sport.

Achieving clarity about who you are, what you have to offer and what you want, are of course all linked and that meant taking a few hits and reality checks. I persisted.

Just quietly—I met the love of my life on E-Harmony!

JUST FOR LAUGHS,
FILL OUT AN ON-LINE
DATING PROFILE. GO ON,
IT'S ENLIGHTENING AND FUN.

NO NEED TO MAKE IT LIVE.

# I WAS ROYALLY CALLED OUT!

## Relationship #6—Surround Yourself With Honesty

Meetings are not my favourite thing. This one was called, by me I might add, to discuss finalising the new company website before it went live. The agenda was all about the detail; have we ticked every box, checked all the links, proofed and double-proofed the page copy and ensured the sales funnels worked? Probably the closest I get to my idea of a living nightmare, but... I knew how important it was. I also did not want to look sloppy or unprofessional at the launch.

I headed into the meeting with four others and another on SKYPE ready to contribute and get it signed off. 'Right, let's get on with it!" All energy and bluster in my tone.

We started in a flurry of ideas and note taking. Everyone jostled for air as they added their 10cents worth. It went on for 90 minutes... 90 extremely long minutes—sigh). The rigorous to-and-fro continued on gritty subjects such as automated emails, database reporting functions and ecommerce capabilities. NIGHTMARE!

I'm what you might call a little bit hands-off. Super at delegating the detail, pretty happy to brainstorm ideas, but not so great in long term logistical discussion forums otherwise known as meetings. Ok, I am rubbish at the detail, I know it... we all know it.

I was really trying. Seriously, I was...

I'll back track a little. We were around 45 minutes in and my resolve was fading. "What should my next blog be about?" and "Ooh that's a great idea for a new 20 second video" and "What shoes should I wear to the movies tonight?" and "Choc top or crisps?" were occupying my thoughts.

"Hang on, hang on," a commanding, rather direct Dutch accent boomed, "Kirsty has seen something sparkly on the floor." Sprung! An eruption of laughter ensued.

A laptop fell awkwardly as the newest member of the team fumbled, aghast at the cheek of the outburst. That was my Tanja, a wonderful colleague and close friend of many years. My reality checker, my rock, my unfaltering confidante, calling me out. I love the people I work with.

Note my choice of words, "work with". It was purposeful. The antiquated hierarchical workplace of the 80s and 90s is just that, driven by fear and retribution from 'The Boss'. Traditionally workplaces were intolerant, inflexible and unstable.

Hiring like-minded, experienced, smart people creates a much flatter work structure. We all have different strengths and we support each other through transparency and good old-school open communication.

Whoever is best to lead a project does, and we all fall into step behind them—or should that be beside? One of my reasons for going into business was to create a positive, supportive culture where each person felt valued. You will read more about culture in the chapter 'Re-Write The Story Of You—At Work'.

I tell the 'something sparkly on the floor' story because it highlights our core business culture: valuing and empowering everyone, no matter their job description.

It's ok to be assertive; coupled with respect, it is a confident method of communicating. So go for it, call me out. It makes me proud of the culture we have achieved.

WHO DO YOU TRUST
TO TELL YOU THE TRUTH
CONSTRUCTIVELY,
NO MATTER WHAT?

PERHAPS THEY ARE
A POSSIBLE MENTOR?

Everything is undeniably about relationships and while building short and long-term relationships might seem a natural way of traversing day-to-day life for some, for others it may not come quite as easily. For me, peeling back the colours that have shaded my ability to interact in real ways with others was an enlightening process.

Discarding preconceptions and taking people as I found them, was in hindsight the only real change I had to make. Ego, comparisons and bias were sidelined by taking that one step. When I think about all of the interesting people I unknowingly walked past in life, what a waste.

Writing this chapter helped me define my Chameleon colours, at the same time, erasing a few shades I no longer needed. Here are four colours that now make up my spectrum.

First up is **grey**. I play the subject not the person. Seeing the world as grey and not black and white has helped immeasurably. It negates the need to be right and creates illuminating discussions, even during disagreements.

I now talk to anyone **(pink)**, which can annoy or embarrass the people I am with. The flipside of being a chronic over sharer? People are interesting, I am curious and my true friends get over it.

**Red** = rude. I have a short attention span and I know it. Disinterest is rude and I need to manage that better.

I exclude people who appear negative **(black)**, thus retaining energy to give to those who are inspirational and good for me.

Nobody communicates appropriately or effectively with everyone all the time. But I think it is worth the risk to talk to everyone you can with an open honest approach. The alternative is a little bland.

IF EVERYTHING
IS ABOUT RELATIONSHIPS,
THINK ABOUT WHAT DEFINES
YOU IN RELATIONSHIPS.

ALLOCATE EACH
ONE A COLOUR.

# CHAPTER 4

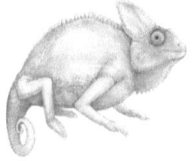

# What the Heck are Hacks?

*"Hack refers to any trick, shortcut,
skill or novelty method that increases
productivity and efficiency in all walks of life."*

Google

## HELPFUL HACKS

I PROVIDED THE DEFINITION of a hack in the contents page at the beginning of this section so I won't elaborate on that. Not a new concept but one that provides bite-sized pieces of wisdom that can be easily digested, as opposed to the time invested in reading an entire book or paper on a subject.

The aim of a Hack, for me anyway, is to provide a shot in the arm when floundering or procrastinating. To bring me back to my goal, mission or project; a 'go to' that causes action. It reframes my thinking when I have been bombarded with the enormous data dump of opinions or information we are exposed to minute by minute in our highly internet based, overly-connected world. The phrases themselves serve to remind me of the message or messages contained within the larger scope of the Hack.

The story of you, I suggest, would be advanced by grabbing hold of at least five Hacks that help you on a regular basis. They can be many things, from a humorous retort to extricate yourself from a sticky situation, to a more serious life management Hack.

Don't try and recognise a Hack, and think, oh, that's a Hack; just pick them up as you go along. I found this one recently and loved it: *'Turn your car seat warmers on to keep your pizza hot on the way home'*. I had literally never thought of this idea.

There are a frenzy of feel good posts in the form of MEMES, designer quotes and poetry floating about in the cybersphere. I know, I write them. We are inundated with them, and yet I use them and save them, they are on my bulletin board, my phone and stored on Instagram. Do you?

While they are an excellent ever-present reminder about keeping a positive attitude and help your mindset, they themselves do very little apart from making you think. Provoking thought is good, it's a start but it doesn't get anything done that takes motion. Actions are the key; actions make a difference. Actions create tangible outcomes.

### Actions drive change

The following pages are an assortment of what I call *'Action Hacks'.*

# HACK 1 — SMASH IT OUT

My first Action Hack: 'Smash it out', whatever 'it' is.

Don't worry if you are unsure of where you are going, how good you will be or what the end game is, just start smashing it and you will figure 'it' out as you go along.

Lately I've been trying 'Action Mantras' to help me smash it out. And yes, I am simply adding action to these existing concepts and I will tell you why. I feel a tad airy fairy saying mantra, and when I add the word action, I feel more purposeful and less fairyful.

So I thought no judgement, try it. I then realised I already used mantras most days. Some of my go-tos you might recognise: 'act now', 'handle each piece of paper once', or 'phone a friend' and 'walk away'. All of which fall into the Action Mantra category, and are what we call in marketing terms, 'a call to action'.

While they help to manage the traps of indecision most of us fall into, reducing the occurrence of procrastination, they become more than that. Used often enough, they become part of your self-management and motivation style. Part of defining your story.

When I find myself over-thinking something, I very rarely keep it to myself; my partner is frequently on the receiving end of my ruminations. His solid go-to retort is "Smash it out Kirsty." A verbal slap upside the head that jolts me out of my introspection. Otherwise the roundabout keeps circling and I cling on, afraid to jump off. Being in my head is a safer space.

I recall a story about my wonderfully quick, well-humoured

nine-year-old nephew. He also falls into the 'over-thinker' category. A little while back, he was in the car with his mum on his way to his first ever NAPLAN school exam. For those who are not in the Primary School World, NAPLAN is The National Assessment Program – Literacy and Numeracy. A series of tests focused on basic skills that are administered annually to Australian students.

Whilst nobody is under the illusion that these tests might be something to look forward to, the car was unusually quiet. Even his six-year-old sibling, who I would describe as 'born to perform' and who I'm told, sings religiously enroute to school, was curiously quiet.

My sister glanced into the rear vision mirror at her eldest son. "You ok? You are rather quiet, what are you thinking?"

My nephew replied, "I think I will do OK today, but I'm a bit nervous."

Mum took a moment and said, "It's good to be nervous, it means you care about doing your best. Now, what would your Uncle David say?" (he's the cool long-haired surfy uncle).

His face lit up with a beaming smile. He yelled "SMASH IT OUT!"

The usual car karaoke resumed, interspersed with a chorus of "smash it outs" at appropriate melodic moments.

And... smash it out he did.

Mantra + Call To Action = Job Done

## HACK 2—FORGET ABOUT THE DETAILED PLAN

One super popular fitness guru was heard to say, "Forget about the plan and Just F...ing Do It!" What an awesome call to action right up there with 'smash it out'. I was in an auditorium the first time I heard it, the chant went up around the room, "JFDI! JFDI! JFDI!" I remember it vividly, a *Marie Claire* Magazine Women's Forum. The room exploded with visceral empowerment, I wanted to leap from my chair and get started that very minute. If only I could bottle that feeling to drag out each time the noise of life interrupted my fervour. "How long would this sensation last?" I wondered. "How many of the hundreds in attendance actually went on to do it?" Whatever 'it' was.

Outside the inspiration of the masses, back inside my day-to-day life I am frequently alone. Sitting in the spare bedroom of our townhouse, the one that serves as my office. Those are the times when I wish like crazy I had that elixir of fervour neatly bottled in a take-home pack, ready to use. Instead I silently and sternly berate myself, "What are you waiting for?" Only to receive the same response time and again, "Fear, I'm waiting for the fear to pass."

I know fear as well as anyone and I have a big, bold kick up the behind sitting on my bulletin board staring me down, not letting me escape. Reminding me with a visual 'shout' that I have to act each and every time fear pokes its infectious, infuriating negativity inside my head. It says:

"Be afraid and do it anyway."

There's that mantra thing again. Playing on repeat like a stuck motivational podcast. A few false starts, that's always my path, I accept that. Eventually I am guided or cajoled into doing 'it'. And that is a tidy segue into my next story.

This is a story about a couple of friends, talented, smart, savvy friends who both desperately want to go out on their own and start a business. The three of us have talked about it for years, yet we are still having the same revolving conversation. Both of them just can't seem to get started. I mean, they have ideas, good ideas and I don't doubt their desire one little bit. Why would they stay working for managers who frustrate them, employers who don't care about them or in roles that limit their obvious talent?

So what's stopping them? The same thing that stops me, really—the need to have everything planned out perfectly, risk mitigated up the wahzoo. In other words, fear! Fear of failure, fear of criticism, of standing out or being different or perhaps it is even more basic, fear of just not being good enough. Living with fear of any kind is crippling, it means you have a degree of pain that you desperately want to transcend. It can feel as if nobody else has those exact feelings, they are peculiar to you. But I am just as certain that they are not. We all have them, and just as I know that, I also know most of us offer excuses that validate our fear and serve to hold us in those patterns of inaction.

In my experience, once that pain is big enough, action will follow. My friends' pain has not reached that point; if it had they would get the hell out of their comfort zone and take the risk.

Easier said than done and there is zero judgement in that preceding statement. I fight that fear and pain most weeks. On Monday I'm queen of the world! Come Thursday, I'm battling with "what the heck do I know, why would anyone come to me for help?" fear talk.

It is that dramatic and that regular.

The difference between us? I know through experience that those feelings of self-doubt will pass, they always do. So I ride it out, sometimes with the help of a quiet beverage and not so quiet rant to my guy.

I have become accustomed to the highs and lows, the wins and losses, the risk and reward of business. I now believe, no matter what, I will be ok, things will happen, I will survive both growth and change and history serves to reinforce that. A history my friends have not experienced and therefore do not have stored away in their 'life armoury'.

My life armoury is a big part of my confidence and resilience. After all, it increases with each challenge I survive. Sometimes it is just that—survival. The plan wasn't perfect, not everything worked, but I/we kept moving.

Of course, I impart this hard-earned wisdom to my friends. More than that, together we nut out objectives and brainstorm ideas. We make each other accountable through checking in and reviewing goals. Still, the leap into full blown action on their part hangs in mid-air. The intellect is willing but the flesh is stationary; it's now obvious it has to be more than fear alone holding them back.

This is what I see. These beautiful beings have some obvious commonalities that could perhaps shed some light. Both are analytical, both are expertly organised, both are perfectionists.

Perfectionists about how they present themselves to the world. Their hair and clothing are managed down to the last detail, they always present beautifully. Their homes are the same, gorgeously on-trend, thoughtfully styled, highly organised. And tidy, very, very tidy most of the time. If they are managing a project, it is done with great attention to detail and forethought. If perfectionists know the end goal they can manage the process effectively and efficiently and ensure the standard is met, often exceeded.

I love this quality, I wish I could claim it. On top of perfectionism let's add 'analytical'. Analytical people look at things from all sides over and over again, especially things in the 'grey zone'.

They often prefer the true or false, right or wrong and black and white of life. The grey zone has no absolutes, it has too many variations or possibilities and becomes a polarising and paralysing minefield.

The analytical perfectionist has two inbuilt hurdles to the inevitable risk of entrepreneurship. This business game is about risk, reacting to the unknown, not having all the answers and rolling with constantly moving goalposts. The long-term plan that can be steadily worked towards, where the goals are clear and organised is not the entrepreneur's world. The entrepreneur is breaking new ground, often going where no one has gone before. Making it up as they go along, so to speak.

When the end of the plan seems nowhere in sight, and there are no rules or processes announcing 'do this next' or perhaps realising there is no right way or perfect way, the analytical perfectionist simply stops—mid leap. What they have done to date is precise and beautiful, but that is where it ends. Rather than keeping the vision as the key driver, it is lost to the perfectionist's need for plans, control and absolutes. It's wonderful to have an idea or a vision, never stop having those. Being detailed and diligent is a strength, albeit one that needs to be managed.

**Combine it with the courage to get started, the tenacity to continue and the resilience to ride out the hiccups and it's a winning formula.**

When things don't go as expected or roadblocks appear (that I can guarantee), all you have to do is make one decision at a time. That's all. Ditch the big long-term, highly structured plan, replace it with a general guide and make sure you celebrate key milestones. Things, life, business, will continue to progress and change based on making that one decision at a time.

Did they get past those perfectionist roadblocks? I hear you wonder. It's a work in progress, but then, what isn't?

HOW ABOUT THROWING
THE WHOLE IDEA OF
A PLAN OUT THE
NEAREST WINDOW?

WHAT IS THE ONE
STEP/DECISION
YOU CAN TAKE TODAY?

## HACK 3—BE REAL

Showering is by far my favourite thing. My best raw and rallying speeches arrive in the shower. If we are in a rush to get somewhere, then do not let me say "I just need a quick shower." I run the water a little too hot, on super full torpedo blast phase and stand there, for ages, turning and thinking. Turning, turning, turning; thinking, thinking, thinking. It's my thinking time, you may have gathered. Well, you can't do much else in the shower, can you?

"I can't get out," my conscience secretly chants. The water is calming, luxurious, and I lose track of time. Suddenly I hear a faint Aussie twang murmur from downstairs, "You said you'd only be 10 minutes... mutter mutter." Was that him? I'm not sure, he does have a habit of talking to himself, I conveniently ignore it and continue my daydream.

Two minutes pass, then boom! "GET OUT!", he yells at full volume from the first floor landing. "I can't!" I hit back.

Knowing full well I have to. My response elicits a few extra moments of heaven.

As I mentioned my best speeches have all taken shape in the shower, they are clear and uncomplicated, raw and real. I can rarely duplicate that level of articulate clarity as it occurs during the first round of my 'shower speech'.

I often say it out loud, as if commanding my audience of shampoo and body wash sitting at attention along the cubicle shelf. I thrive on a silent audience where mistakes go unnoticed and only imagined applause and nods of agreement are forthcoming.

These speeches are one of the few things (apart from David) that can remove me from my shower at speed. Trying desperately not to forget my thoughts I flick the shower off and race dripping into the office to grab my recorder; well, in the early days it was a recorder, now my iPhone does the job seamlessly. I have to get this out, I know it will never be as good if I wait. Already the flow of thought is fading. Hurry, hurry!

There is one other venue that produces great content, usually in the form of 'one-liners'. That is... bed. 3am in bed to be precise.

No matter how comfortable I feel, how dark or chilly it is outside the covers, I am compelled to get up. If only that could be said about the actual time I am supposed to rise each morning. Sometimes I will email myself a note, peering across at David to see if the flash of light as the phone comes alive wakes him. I must record this, however I do it; it has to be now, it has to be straight away.

The clarity and simplicity of thought that appears at 3am in the pitch black of night or while luxuriating in a scalding hot shower, will not wait until I sit comfortably in front of my laptop. The moment is most often lost, the mess of the day getting in the way of that lucid uncomplicated realness.

For me, realness trumps perfection every time.

I bet you've watched those over-produced, schmick marketing videos where the makeup and lighting are perfect and the content is heavily scripted. Think selfie promos or Insta fashionistas styled beyond all grasp of the average person.

They're not for me, as they evoke no feelings at all.

They seem more focused on looking good, the production itself and their image than relating to what matters to the listener. The realness is masked, the sales pitch too obvious; in other words, it is more about them than the audience.

People relate to people, real people, people they find a connection with who are imperfect and relentlessly genuine. Something often forgotten as we fire off emails and texts at a great rate of knots. Creating real connections is difficult when we rely solely upon technology to communicate.

Real connection takes a combination of our senses. When well aligned with our story, the outcome will be one that creates trust. A trust that is lost in over-produced, expertly managed posts, webinars and podcasts.

The challenge before us all is to share something of ourselves, emote, make mistakes, show our imperfections, be authentic. They are part of each of us, perhaps our insecurities are the very things that form that link with another person. Often our most guarded secrets, the things that make us the most vulnerable are where the power to connect resides.

Finding that real voice will be different for each of us, the level of openness to commit to might be the hardest thing, how far does one go? Being open and vulnerable whilst keeping one eye on the objective. Nobody wants to be that chronic over-sharer. However, consider the alternative. A guarded existence where no criticism is leveled, small talk reigns supreme and acquaintances are your only companions.

UNMASK YOUR CHAMELEON

COULD YOU MAKE A SHORT
'REAL YOU' VIDEO
USING YOUR PHONE?

PERHAPS FIRST THING
IN THE MORNING, NO MAKEUP,
HAIR A MESS, POOR LIGHTING,
JUST THE REAL YOU AND
YOUR IDEAS OR THOUGHTS.

THEN MAKE IT PUBLIC—EEEEK!

## HACK 4—NEUTERING NASTY STUFF

Living life is not a solo proposition. It is one that means we come into contact with people who disagree with us and the odd asshole. Situations will occur that we have no control over, we will all fail and we will all face criticism. That's a given. The challenge is how to re-frame those negative events in a constructive light.

When compiling this chapter I thought, "which of those areas should I draw on to illustrate my point?" There are a great many negatives swilling around in my head to choose from: death, divorce, infertility, failed business partnerships, illness, redundancy... sigh, a lot. I settled on failure.

In all fairness, no matter which story I decide to tell the message is going to be the same.

**How you react to any particular event comes down to you. That decision will set you up for a positive or negative attitude and in due course, have bearing on both the outcome itself and how you think and feel about yourself.**

I'll pick divorce, ever the fun-filled adventure. Some years ago I separated from my thoroughly English husband, let's call him 'the first husband'. Two years later the divorce was final. I won't go into the variety of issues that perpetuated the split and eventual divorce; it was complex, it was messy, it was emotional. All to be expected. I won't go into it because early on in the process I decided that it would not define me, I would not be the quintessential 'anti-men divorcée'.

I decided to shield my psyche from the fallout that is reliving the event each time it was told. To me, that just kept the tumultuous emotions alive and thriving. To do that I needed a phrase, one that could shut down any and all probing or intrusive questions pertaining to the subject. I landed on this:

**"I am amicably divorced."**

To my relief, this did indeed shut down most conversations around said subject. It also served to leave me feeling positive about the manner in which we had both conducted ourselves during that time. It certainly didn't revive any of those old negative feelings. Ultimately I used it enough that it is now the overriding emotion I have around the entire event. I say it with pride and an unwavering confidence, my decision has benefited my attitude and my management of the process long term.

Modifying your thinking and reactions, especially in negative situations, is difficult. Most of us have an 'auto response' button, phrases or reactions we trot out in certain circumstances. Phrases we have put in place at one time or another as armour. But sometimes those automated reactions have waned in their effectiveness. Recognising the ones that no longer work for you may occur organically, at other times your 'people' may take it upon themselves to point them out. Either way, neither may result in changing that behaviour easily or immediately.

Habitual responses build up over years and for a while they might have worked well. This kind of change takes some managing and a whole load of self-honesty.

The 'Ice Maiden' of my past now smiles readily and makes eye contact. The post-40 divorcée remembers the good times and there were many. The introvert who sought the company and excitement of drama queens has been sidelined, now revelling in calm consistency.

If you have recognised that a particular behaviour is not eliciting an effective outcome:

1. Decide to change that behaviour and
2. Commit to an action that supports the change.

It won't happen overnight, but it will happen.

Just as we discussed in **'Smash It Out'**.

WHAT 'NASTY STUFF'
HAVE YOU EXPERIENCED
THAT YOU NEED TO RE-FRAME?

WHAT NEW LANGUAGE
CAN YOU PUT AROUND
THAT EXPERIENCE?

# HACK 5—FALL IN LOVE WITH FAILURE

I am going to talk about two people who taught me a lot. I have to include a couple of pilots here, or soon-to-be pilots. These two in particular taught me lessons in persistence, positivity and how I, as a business owner as well as personally, react to failure.

The catalyst was a candidate asking for a refund. He had failed to gain a cadetship. My first reaction was shock—we work hard for our candidates and this doesn't happen. Shock quickly turned to self-doubt, even after 18+ years in this industry and thousands of success stories across the world. But as you know, that's the expected and normal emotional reaction most of us experience with any sort of failure.

I followed my protocol (or as we say in aviation, my SOPs – standard operating procedures), and after I had calmed the heck down, I spoke with my most trusted colleague. I knew she would react with fact-based and practical action. She said, "Right, put your management plan into action and make this work for you and your client." She was right, I could use this as an opportunity to provide an even better service. So I did, I gave a full refund immediately but I decided to go further. I wanted to do everything possible to offer support to this candidate and help him manage this career hiccup.

Next was the offer of a complimentary 30-minute 'debrief'. The debrief was to help him get past this feeling of failure and into the right mindset to start thinking about Plan B. During this process I am usually able to pinpoint which areas of the recruitment process need more work and how I can help the candidate to improve. I also suggested another hour of coaching prior to his next interview, at no charge. I wanted to provide more tools and support so he could put a new career plan into action and look at the alternatives open to him. There are always alternatives. The response I received was upset, anger and lashing out. In fact, he blamed everyone, the SIM (flight simulator) trainer, me, the technical information he was provided. He said none of it helped him. I kept reaching out but sadly did not hear from him again.

Fast forward to another cadet six months later, he too had failed to gain a place in his preferred pilot cadet program. This aspiring pilot had done a tonne of work to prepare for the most highly-contested cadet program in the country. He had great potential, passion and commitment to this career path and the work he knew it required. At the time he was only 18, fresh out of high school, with no on-the-job experience. I had prepared him right from the start that airlines have to be really sure a cadet has enough life experience and maturity to commit to this long-term process. Explaining this was often a hard sell to a new school leaver. This time around, it proved to be the case.

The airline didn't offer him a place in the program. They did say, go away, work for a year, gain some life experience and come back. Was he upset? Of course he was, devastated to be frank. He rang me and exploded in hyper conversation. I listened as he got it all off his chest. We proceeded to talk it through and I remember telling him that this airline actually meant it when they said they want to see him again. They could see his potential and he should listen to that. We then made a plan for the next 12 months.

He said, "Ok, I'm going to get a job and get my hands dirty and save up to get this flying career one way or another!"

Twelve months later on the dot, he came back. Not just to say he was giving it another go, but to start his preparation all over again with the new wealth of knowledge he had gained about himself. I asked him what he had learnt on the building site and he said:

*"I learnt to take orders.*

*I learnt that no job was too small or too unimportant for me to do.*

*I learnt that I can work with tradespeople or talk to multi-millionaire owners.*

*I learnt that I could pick up new concepts and ideas quickly.*

*I learnt what hard work is."*

So, round two cadet program interviews—he got the place!

I feel exceptionally privileged that when his dad asked him what he wanted to do to prepare for this second attempt, he said, "I just need to talk to Kirsty." I am lucky enough to have shared his entire journey from first hurdle until today, when I see his Facebook posts as he flies as a First Officer on a Turbo Prop aircraft around Australia.

What I saw, the airline saw, his tenacity, motivation, confidence and resilience.

How you respond to failures or hiccups in your career and personal life is pivotal to riding out the hard times and relishing the good ones. Nothing in life is guaranteed but how you choose to react is totally within your power.

WHETHER IT IS YOURSELF
OR THE OTHER PARTY WHO ARE
UNREASONABLE, IRRATIONAL
OR WRONG, IT IS WORTH
REMEMBERING THAT IT IS
IMPOSSIBLE TO HAVE A
RATIONAL CONVERSATION WITH
AN IRRATIONAL PERSON.

INCLUDING YOURSELF.

LET THE EMOTIONAL RESPONSE
DIE DOWN AND ONLY THEN
DECIDE ON THE NEXT STEPS.

FAILURE IS OUR GREATEST TEACHER.

WHAT HAVE YOU LEARNED ABOUT
YOURSELF FROM YOUR FAILURES?

# HACK 6 — BE CHEEKY

Picture this: a young 20-something Kiwi girl arrives in a glittering new seaside town, ready for a fresh start. She has fled a controlling relationship and travelled across the Nullarbor Desert (technically called a 'Plain' it is arid and looks way more like a Desert to most) to rebuild her life on the East Coast of Australia. She must find a job quickly before her small buffer of funds dwindles to nothing.

Rejection after rejection, she doesn't have that particular industry experience, her CV appears nomadic and employers assume she lacks commitment and stability. Her office skills are average. Ok, self-pep talk... she has always paid her way and will find something, keep at it, try something different, think outside the box. Like most mornings, she is on the Net wandering through screeds of job boards when for some reason a Drake Personnel job advertisement catches her eye. General Office Manager/Receptionist wanted, no industry experience required, suit good all-rounder. It was local too, only one suburb away.

"Perfect," she thinks.

Application sent, she waits for a response. La la la, ho hum, waiting, waiting waiting. Nothing comes... so she decides to give them a call. Getting past the receptionist might be tough. Receptionist: "We've had literally..." dragging that word out like it's never ending, "hundreds of applications so you will just have to wait until we process them and get to you."

"Ok," she thinks, hanging up. Next day, nothing.

She decides it is worth looking a little pushy and calls again.

"Hi, I called yesterday, just wondering if I can talk to the consultant in charge of this role."

"No, Janet is too busy, in fact we have decided to cut applications so if you have not been issued an interview then you have missed out on this one."

Down goes the phone. "Hmmm," she thinks, "I'm not taking that, but how do I get around this gatekeeper?" She researches the names of the Drake consultants and finds one called Janet. Guess what? Her last name is Douglas, what are the odds, maybe she is a relative? She calls one last time realising that she has not given the gatekeeper her full name. "Hi, it's Casey Douglas here, Janet's cousin, can I have a quick word?" She is put straight through. "Woohoo, now just make a damn impression," she thinks. Janet picks up the phone "You are not my bleeping cousin but you have balls so I will give you three minutes."

Needless to say, she had made herself memorable. From the first moment Janet met her, she knew she would get the role.

A big part of forging ahead in life and in your career, is getting a fair go, being given an opportunity or having someone else take a risk on you. What if nobody gives that to you? Life isn't fair. But keep waiting for it to happen and you'll be doing just that—waiting.

Take back some of that control and attempt to create some opportunities. There will be many gatekeepers ahead to outsmart.

**View them as a challenge.**

NOBODY WILL MAKE A DIFFERENCE BY SIMPLY DOING THE SAME THINGS THE SAME WAY AS EVERYONE ELSE.

WHO ARE YOUR GATEKEEPERS?

HOW WILL YOU CREATE OPPORTUNITIES TO GET AROUND THEM?

## HACK 7—MATURE EGO VERSUS EGO MANIAC

What is a 'mature ego' and why should we cultivate one? First up ego is not a dirty word; even if a little self-serving, we all need one. I will admit that Ego Maniac as a description is a tad brutal, so let's change that to mature versus immature ego, and look at why it pays to understand ego pros and cons.

A mature ego means you are likely to be much better at self-managing your emotions. You will also be solution focused rather than getting all caught up in the drama of situations. A somewhat simplified description but one that works for these purposes.

I'll hijack a phrase from one of the largest companies in Australia who describes Ego Maturity as: "A sound level of self-confidence with an overriding graciousness."

Simply put, **be confident but nice!**

A mature ego is a life skill, this is why I encourage its cultivation.

**How to spot a Mature Ego:**

- Likes to mentor and support others.
- Sees other people's point of view.
- Seeks to learn and improve.
- Leads by setting a great example.
- Not afraid to do little jobs as well as big ones.
- Has a high degree of self-knowledge.
- Admits faults and mistakes.
- Takes responsibility for their actions.
- Creates solid relationships.
- Focuses on solutions.

Learning to recognise an immature ego is just as important. Notice the dude telling the entire room how smart he/she is. Watch for the person trying to take over the conversation or task. Yes, you have possibly spotted one. I would also stay away from those who are overly critical or gossipy as this kind of behaviour infects and influences by stealth.

**Here's how you might spot a few characteristics of the immature ego:**

- Defensive when makes mistakes.
- A 'right-fighter,' someone who needs to be right all the time.
- Does not take direction well.

- Sulks or becomes aggressive in communication style.

- Repeats mistakes or does not learn from the past easily.

- Does not listen.

- Blames others.

- Does not show empathy.

Every one of us has come into contact with people who fall into the immature ego category. Even if not obvious at first, patterns tend to expose themselves over time. Now, that doesn't mean they cannot or will not make the move over to the mature side. For me, it means that during their life experience thus far, they have not needed or been required to rewrite those attributes and attitudes. They have not had strong enough influencers who encourage or inspire them to do so.

If something works, it will be repeated until it stops working. Immature egos continue to use those tactics. More often than not, they are getting the result they desire. Nobody should be written off simply because they have yet to progress past those traits. Seek to positively influence those immature egos by how you conduct yourself.

Don't go losing ego all together, but let's try not to put up with too many of those Kanye moments.

HOW WOULD YOU ATTEMPT TO CONSTRUCTIVELY INFLUENCE AN IMMATURE EGO?

WHAT MATURE EGO ASSETS DO YOU NEED TO CULTIVATE A LITTLE MORE?

# HACK 8—TENACITY AND RESILIENCE ARE YOUR BEST FRIENDS

I wholeheartedly attribute the joint traits of tenacity and resilience as being the core drivers that got me to where I am in life right now. Having been accused, albeit within a complimentary delivery, of being lucky to be in my own business, I felt compelled to ask myself was any of it luck? The assumption appeared to be that this thing called luck got me here and that in being your own boss and making your own rules, life has to be easier. Interesting assumption.

Well, while I wouldn't be anywhere else, luck had little to do with it and being the boss is anything but easy. Clearly I need to whinge more about the challenges, although some may say I am quite vocal on that account already.

When you kick off a business you wear every hat: I.T. Guru; Marketing Manager; New Business Development; Accounts and Strategist. Let alone working on the tools, aka doing the work itself.

What I think the word luck refers to is having a role you care about and making it into something that supports your life. That's a perspective I relate to more.

Remember early on I had a kind of drive, it was a niggling unease, constantly reminding me that I was meant to create something bigger than just me. I always said, **"I know I am meant to do something however I am not quite sure what that is."**

I tried different things, working diligently, taking risks. Three failed partnerships ensued, three different business ideas I poured myself into, none of which panned out. Some friendships were reframed, money was scattered to the hemisphere and confusion was a constant state of being.

Still that feeling haunted me—I was meant to do something.

Last year was my 18th year in business, it has gone by in a flash. We had achieved the biggest growth in our history, up by a whopping 30%. I reinvested everything back into the business, enabling us to get the right help to increase automation, hire and train new coaches, redesign another website, the fourth, and much more.

At the end of a 12-month frenzy of activity, we had achieved most of what we had set out to do. I was exhausted. I was also overwhelmed with pride at the result. We had repositioned the business and could now reach an even larger share of the market. Full automation had in fact changed us from a domestic service provider to an international one. The super long 16-hours days were a thing of the past. Our new systems ensured we managed our day-to-day activities more effectively and efficiently.

Finding the right coaches was a godsend. Another light bulb lit up when I realised that I was not the only person who could coach in this specialised environment. My ego was thoroughly checked, my old school thinking reframed for today's obstacles and opportunities. It was this very thinking that had been holding me back, limiting both myself and the business. My role should be to set my team up to succeed through training and support systems, not to hand hold and hover. It was a redefining moment for sure.

My partner used to say to me, "I don't know how you kept up that pace for that long, and you only fell apart twice!" Thanks, hon.

Whatever each of us decides to do, it won't be easy. If it were, everyone would be doing it. The next time someone said to me, you are so lucky to be your own boss, I smile and say, "Thanks. That's what happens when you dig in and don't give up."

CHAPTER

5

# Re-Write the Story of You at Work

## CAREER—WHAT IF I JUST HAVE A JOB?

CALL IT A JOB OR A CAREER—it's 'same, same'. Why get caught up in the semantics? Any role that you do well, are committed to and probably enjoy could be called either. You make it into a career if you choose to.

It is less about status and education. Instead we might classify a career as a pursuit that is authentically defined by two actions:

**learning** and **progression**. Careers are created from any single job dependent upon your attitude towards it and what you decide to accomplish with it.

You may not have a high flying position or what may be considered the 'right' job. Perhaps it is not even something you are passionate about. But it *is* a job, so the question has to be:

## What am I going to do with it?

As much as I admire Dr Martin Luther King Jr. and despite that fact that he is one of my influencers, his "I Have A Dream" speech leaves many of us at a loss. I didn't have a dream, did you?

For those who did, perhaps right out of school—good for you, what a great kick-start. The rest of us have to try things, take risks and get out there to find something.

There are careers that exist now that simply did not when some of us were at school or university. You may have your own ideas, some of which could be turned into a business. Businesses that can be started from home, in a bedroom, a garage or on the dining room table. Online tools and easy website creation mean anyone can build a presence and access markets domestically and internationally from anywhere. Talk about world and oyster, it's so true. The web has liberated our options and those options are now endless.

In my little corner of the world, I started with one accidental client and I continued to work part time in recruitment for several years. Five years passed more quickly than I realised and my part time coaching gig had expanded to coaching pilots around Australia, New Zealand and Asia. Now we are on our third business model, fifth web design reinvention and the business has gained a degree of relative success. We coach pilots and cabin crew for 45 airlines worldwide, all via our on-line SKYPE-based preparation program. The entire business is virtual and run through automation. The interesting thing is, I had no concept when I started that coaching would end up looking like this.

When I started, automation wasn't an option, but then that's half the excitement, having to continually learn and adapt and respond to the market as well as your own needs. Accepting evolution and remaining flexible is critical in navigating business and creating a workable work/lifestyle. Embracing change is a skill, one I wish I had realised earlier. Rather than dwelling on that late start, I acknowledge that it's never too late to start anything or accept the lessons provided by trying.

If you find yourself reading this and thinking, "I don't have any qualifications," "I have no time," "I'm too old," "I don't have enough money" or "There is nowhere to go in this role," then nothing at all will change. Continuing to do the same things, expecting a different outcome? You know the rest.

## If you want change then change something, anything

Imagine this 35-year-old, head down in the spare bedroom. Clients came to my home and sat at my Ikea dining table or stood in my kitchen while I whipped up a cuppa. Moreover, my personal circumstances did nothing to reinforce that this was in fact the right time to start anything. I was single, had minimal savings and no assets. What was I thinking? On top of that my formal education ceased at the end of High School. Well, I was thinking why not? I loved coaching, "let's see where it takes me."

In hindsight a little naivety was a good thing. Had I known the hurdles, challenges and failures ahead it may have proved demoralising. Looking back on those first years I am amazed how much I learned as each problem was solved. Pretty proud of getting through it and surviving the dreaded five-year mark, when statistically new business fails.

It took that full five years before coaching could support me. At the 10-year mark, another hurdle presented itself, my imminent divorce. That one uncomfortable event kicked me quite literally into serious business mode, after all it would be my sole income (talk about motivation). Divorce was the catalyst that has seen this business grow to employ others, become an industry leader and expand worldwide to work in over 20 countries. Who knew that would happen? Not me, that's for sure. I know you've noticed that negative motivation concept pop up again here, the big "D". It sure seems to work for me as far as propelling action is concerned.

As you will have gathered by now, I remain sceptical of those all-encompassing proclamations such as 'finding your purpose or passion' and 'finding happiness' or indeed any of those mountainous life-goal style sayings. 'One foot in front of the other', 'You only have now', 'What are you going to do with it?' are more my style.

Having already discussed the paralysing effects the enormity of finding your life purpose exudes, not to mention that perfectionism perpetuates procrastination (that's a mouthful), let's expand our thinking around jobs, careers and the core drivers that lie within us all.

## Your job does not define you

My guy is only too clear that his job is not all he is. He is also super clear on the other stuff he is 'into'. If anyone ridiculously epitomises 'you are not your job', it's him. He'll rail off a list of things that rock his world, things that he will do every chance he gets, to the exclusion of all else, no joke, starting with surfing. We all know what surfers are like: if there is surf, it is going to be a great day. No wait—a freakin' awesome day! He will skip work and leave the front door unlocked as he races to the waves for anything over a 2-foot swell. It's something I live with. What else? Science—if I have to read another post by Neil deGrasse Tyson I'll do it, but with a massive eye roll. Music, new Aussie music. So nope, nothing I can sing to. Just once I'd like a road trip where I can belt out an Adele or GaGa ballad. Not going to happen though, "The Australian new music scene needs our support." Ok, Ok!

As you can see, passion runs strongly in this Surfy-Sciencey guy. There's more, but I think you get the point. That's great for him, but what if you are someone who when asked "What are you in to?" responds with, "I don't really know"? That person where no apparent life purpose or passion has exposed itself, in a job that will never be a career and maybe no regular hobbies. All of which provides fodder for an irrational fear of being asked.

I would suggest that those things do lie within you. The intellectual you has merely failed to define them clearly and therefore you assume they are missing. How about we by-pass the intellectual you and temporarily try to ignore the analytical, fact driven, evidence driven part of you that is perhaps causing a disconnection. What if we ask the emotional you?

Not in an airy fairy way but in a listen-to-what-moves-you way. Bear with me. I'm talking about listening to the things that get your blood boiling, make you cry or rail in anger; the things that make you laugh hysterically or exclaim "that's super cute." Those are your 'I'm into...' things. I bet you don't have to think about those emotions, they just occur randomly in reaction to your world. There are likely to be a combination of day-to-day things and momentous things. It's not all going to be positive; in fact attempting to be positive at all times can be an intellectual response to the traumas and tragedies of life. Positivity may well be a management technique, one that could be part of the problem as it can lead to a state of denial. That denial may cause an inability to connect with all the elements that shape you and what you are in to.

Getting down to the nitty gritty of what authentically moves you, of what you relate to, will involve shedding the nauseating wonderfulness perpetrated by social media that masks real life. So let's not exclude those negative motivations when they may have a purpose.

Where to start with defining those things that evoke an emotional response? I'll kick this thinking off with my list. You will find it on the next page. First up are the categories I used to ensure my list covered a variety of pieces of me:

*The insignificant*

*The serious*

*The life-changing*

*The bold*

*The bad*

*The weird*

*The silly*

## MY 'I'M INTO' LIST

*Baby goats or puppies doing pretty much anything on Insta.*

*My dog and his unconditional love.*

*Splice Ice Blocks and Hokey Pokey ice cream (A Kiwi thing).*

*A rocking pair of shoes, I have about 300.*

*Massages, I just loooooove them, my idea of heaven. (If I end up in the 'Good Place' my hope is they deliver them daily).*

*That tingling feeling after exercise, when I have really pushed myself.*

*Helping or mentoring friends and just about anyone else.*

*Donating to kids in hospital fighting indiscriminate diseases.*

*Fighting famine, abuse and lack of education.*

*Spotlighting social injustice and infertility.*

*Standing against sexual predators, and aggressive, abusive people.*

*Blogging on inequality and racism.*

*Movies that make me laugh and cry uncontrollably.*

*My nephews and their familiar family traits (Smile).*

*Writing about anything and everything.*

*Fresh linen sheets after a warm shower.*

*A Rosé hangover. The best excuse to do nothing all day.*

WRITING YOUR LIST
DOWN MAKES THOUGHTS
TANGIBLE AND SOMEHOW
MORE REAL

WHAT EVOKES AN EMOTIONAL
RESPONSE IN YOU?

MAKE THOSE THINGS YOUR
'I'M INTO' LIST

## THE POWER OF WRITING IT DOWN

That brings me to my next action idea, the physical act of putting thoughts, ideas and feelings down on paper. I'm no psychologist but this process seems to make those things more real, gives them tangibility, a form, a structure.

Writing is a process, one worth taking the time to try. However you write, it is your voice and that voice is unique to you.

I had to relearn the power of this physical act. I was stuck in self-defeatist mode, ego bruised, blue-day type stuck, trying to bring this book together. Squeezing it in among my other life responsibilities, resenting each one as it drew me away from my writing. Scrolling endlessly through my pages of content, sighing, staring at each page, not achieving much. I knew what I wanted to say, why was it so darn difficult to pull together? I just needed some clear uncluttered time, time I never really had. There was always something else pulling at me. Frustration, I now see, turned to avoidance, excuses and justifications. In reality I was procrastinating.

On one such 'avoidance dog-walk' a few sage words imparted by an author acquaintance unexpectedly popped into my head. She had said, "Get a cork board, write each chapter and subject heading on post-it notes and pin them to the board." I thought, "Really? Why would that be any better than having it on my laptop?" Huge doubter, huge! I thanked her for her tip and proceeded to never use it. Bloody know-it-all first time author, I was. Well, I got to the point when I was out of options so reluctantly I placed my ego aside and said, "Why not, I'll give it a crack."

In short, it worked! That little white Kikki K corkboard littered with yellow sticky notes provided a snapshot of the entire project at a single glance, one I easily and quickly referred to when I needed to connect chapters or pieces of copy. This simple visual technique showed me where I was and where I was going. It was that simple and yet that difficult.

My ego had gotten smack dab in the way, another one of those battles I continue to have with myself, another thing I have to relearn over and over again: **an immature ego moment can hold you back.**

Even if you don't have a use for this chapter right now, keep it in the back of your mind for that day when you too are frustrated and need to get out of your own way.

Faced with a period of uncertainty, be that in a career or a personal challenge, I often come back to one question, **"What are you/I motivated by on a day-to-day basis?"** Frequently when I have posed this question I have received the following response, "I don't know what motivates me." That made me think is it really that we don't know, or rather that our motivations have not been given a name, have not been clearly defined?

You've pulled together your 'I'm Into' list so how about we develop that further. What if we had a process to help drag it out from the recesses of the brain? Rather than simply things you are in to, I'm going to move into a more feelings/actions based narrative, the 'What Moves Me To Act' list.

Open questions such as "What motivates you?" appear to have no beginning, no end and no structure, making them feel like a momentous task. So let's not use those questions and be more specific or targeted in our own questions, as they are easier to answer. After all, that is the premise of this entire book—asking the right questions in order to build your story.

**Writing it down is the action phase that precedes the launch phase.** Here we go...

## WHAT MOVES ME TO ACT?

Q1. **If you could do any five things on any one day off, what would they be?**

Q2. **If you are at work, with no particular deadline, what do you choose to do first?**

Q3. **It's your day off again, what are three things you would avoid at all costs?**

Q4. **You are at work, what three things do you dread doing the most?**

Q5. **The last time you cried, what was it in response to?**

Q6. **The last time you laughed uncontrollably was in response to what?**

**Q7.** The last time you felt compelled to comment on Twitter, Insta, LinkedIn or Facebook, what was the discussion?

**Q8.** What was the last thing you donated to or volunteered for?

Have you pulled a few thoughts together? It's ok if it is only a few, there is no right or wrong amount, there is just you and what moves you to act. Nothing you list needs to conform to anyone else's version of what you should or should not be into, or be moved by. This is what rocks your world and yours alone.

Perhaps you see a pattern? Even a small pattern may provide some indication of your core motivations or drivers. Thinking back there have been a couple of people I have been privileged to work with whose stories epitomise this process. They are unforgettable for the fact that they both came from a place where they felt direction-less after suffering significant life hurdles. I'd like to share their stories.

## Awesome Person #1

One of our Cuzzies from over the dutch (aka ditch, which is the Tasman Sea Cuzzies is how New Zealanders and Australians refer to each other), a 50-something who was pretty new to Australia, starting over and a fush outa water (again that's phonetic Kiwi speak for anyone who is unsure—just say it out loud to translate).

She had 30 years experience in hospitality, executive or PA roles and in a previous life had run a successful dairy farm.

A widely experienced candidate, not a specialist in any one area, let's call her a skilled generalist. Her work ethic was outstanding and her references matched that. But she didn't really know what made her unique or how to illustrate her story when up against 200 other candidates for a job, many a lot younger than she. Her confidence needed a reboot and she was up for it.

She had spied an awesome role, Executive PA and host for a very wealthy businessman.

The offer included accommodation. The role: guest relations, office and diary management and being the right hand for this international jet-setter. All from his base in a very sought after beach-side holiday destination. Man, even I wanted this job!

"I won't have a chance," she said.

'Ppppfffftttt," was my response, "let's give it your best shot."

I've referenced her story previously during some of my blogs on career and age, and yes, there are perceived difficulties we need to manage right alongside the benefits of her maturity and life experience.

"Why don't we be totally random?" I said.

Let's give them a taste of what they could expect, literally.

Guess what we did? We used her spectacular culinary skills.

We planned a cocktail event menu, formatting it on luxurious cream 160gsm card. Matching local regional wines to each course.

"Can you cook all of that?" I asked.

"Of course I can," she said, looking a little bemused.

I'm not the best cook and some of these dishes were way beyond my meagre skills. This girl knows her stuff, I thought.

She selected three items to whip up. Along with the ingredients we picked up a small travel sized Esky or you might call it a cooler.

The idea was that along with her fabulous CV and references we'd include this fully planned cocktail event for ten, costed, with samples of three menu items and courier it directly to the powers that be.

Who would dream of receiving an application like that? No one—that's who! Genius! Ok, calm down.

Why don't we drop in a handwritten note saying, "Just to ensure you received my application I will call you on Tuesday at 3pm to talk you through the menu and serving suggestions." There's the 'call to action', not leaving it in their hands, keeping it in ours or hers, I should say. With any luck they will have called before then, which may make the conversation a little easier.

Out of 370 applications from around the country this talented all rounder was one of three short listed candidates and flew up for the final meet and greet four days later.

Job done—love that story.

## Awesome Person #2

This 30-something had a failed retail business. Caught by the economic downturn, he had lost the lot. The brutality of the industry had taken its toll and he couldn't hide his disgust at himself for failing, or his anger at the industry.

Time for a change. Enter the debrief. This helps put the past to bed and refocus on next steps. The plan: once he found a role he really wanted, instead of submitting a standard resumé we decided to pull together a full-on staged product photo shoot. Using their products of course.

Yes! We will treat this as a marketing project, we will also use visual media. Why not do product placement; after all, this is a sales role. We included the actual animal, the one who eats this wonderfully unique kibble. So the pooch or pooches, depending on how many we could bribe into behaving at one time, would be part of the shoot. Hang on—audio, we need audio! We need a video introduction as part of the resumé, perfect. Final touch, case studies: we can quantify the outcomes of several of his past sales projects and present them as case studies.

If you are thinking we went over the top, you are correct. What employer could overlook this type of preparation—sales presentation, graphics plus results? He was the only non-industry salesperson to apply and the youngest candidate. He was also short listed to the top five candidates immediately—woohoo!

Final stage, we ensured he had the key numbers ready on the tip of his tongue in order to wow them with actual results. Not only that, he devised five different marketing strategies based on his industry research and produced a 'Fast Facts Sheet' on how to reinvigorate their products to their current client base and examine new customer niches.

Result: I did mention he was the youngest and least experienced applicant they had, and.... he was welcomed to the team. Well done!

NONE OF THIS INVOLVED
ROCKET SCIENCE. IT INVOLVED
A PROCESS, A FEW IDEAS, RESEARCH,
THE COURAGE TO DO
SOMETHING DIFFERENTLY.

AS WELL AS A SOLID LEVEL
OF BACKING YOURSELF.

YOU MIGHT EVEN CALL IT
SELF-BELIEF.

## REPROGRAM YOUR SELF-BELIEFS

You guessed it, we are about to examine self-belief. I remember with ridiculous vividness how my mum used to accuse me of being lazy. Especially around exam time when my older brother was beavering away with tutors and tests and reading up a storm an entire month in advance, and I wasn't.

I learnt in a different way to him and when 'She Who Must be Obeyed' saw me cramming for school tests last minute, by which I mean the night before, she assumed I didn't work enough during term. Wrong. It was more that if I didn't use it I would lose it, so cramming for me helped bring things to the forefront of my mind, make them fresh again.

High School wasn't exactly difficult for me. Now I am no 'brain' but I could get through with say, a medium effort. An even less observable effort if it was a subject I was interested in, as it seemed to stick. One such subject was History, I loved it, I can still recite the ramifications of Apartheid in South Africa, the Bantu Stands and the mix of European cultures that led to this segregated society. Fascinating stuff to this medium brain. I later realised that parts of history resonated strongly with me and I came to understand what topics and ideas moved me. In this case, social injustice.

The subconscious is an unusual being. It latches onto things it hears over and over again. My subconscious took to that oft repeated 'mum' message, "you are lazy" as fact. It drilled its way into my psyche becoming entrenched as part of who I was, or at least, believed I was. It became generally accepted by those around me, **I was lazy**. That particular belief was perpetrated by a person I loved, so of course it held a lot of power. That's where many self-beliefs start, with authority figures. It's quite cathartic to decide that a once superior being might be wrong.

I remember thinking, "You know what, that could not, let me repeat... could not be further from the truth." She was categorically wrong and I was in need of some reprogramming.

This bandying about of a perceived failure had usurped the facts, it had bullied facts out of the way and replaced them by mesmerizing repetition with a falsehood. That's how slowly and easily false beliefs can occur through repetition. You hear it enough, you believe it. And that, apart from anything else, is annoying. So here we are walking around with all these false self-beliefs as part of our identity. What can we do about it?

First off, we need to re-program our brains or our thinking and just as these intruders drilled themselves in through repetition, it is totally possible to replace them through the very same technique.

In order to do that, you will have to decide what those false self-beliefs are. The 'Perception' chapter that follows will help. Once false self-beliefs have been identified, a repetitive mantra will help kick the change off. I know it sounds a bit mundane but that is how they got in there in the first place.

Here is the re-programming program:

1. *Perform the 'Perception Exercise'.*

2. *Decide which self-beliefs you want to change.*

3. *Replace the false belief with a new "I Am" statement.*

4. *Play on repeat.*

I replaced "I am lazy" with a new version "I work a lot." Not perfectly positive but way closer to the truth. I can deal with the truth in practical terms.

Here I am with this new 'true belief' and although working a lot is not optimum, naming it, and knowing it is real has improved my self-knowledge and self-belief, it has rewritten my internal conversation.

Here's the positive decision out of that discussion.

"I have a great work ethic," might be a nice way to re-frame it.

Being true and factual means this new self-knowledge is a real thing and real things are something that can be worked with. I can and have, not always successfully, put into place management techniques to deal with the negative side effects of working too much.

**It's pretty hard to manage a belief that isn't real.**

In the next chapter we will pursue others in the search for what is true and real about us. Finding out how you are perceived is the first step, let's get on it.

# DO YOU REALLY KNOW HOW YOU ARE PERCEIVED?

## Want to Find Out?

Perception is an interesting phenomenon. We might think we know how we come across to others but are we sure? I thought I was sporty, if you recall earlier in the book, my friend however insisted I was more of a slim person. Pfffftttt.

Our definition of ourselves is one thing, how we are being perceived is quite another.

I don't know about you but I thought I was all over it. This girl knows herself, this girl is all that, putting it out in the world, doing it, making it happen. Nobody knows me like me. I don't care what anyone thinks.

I was in for a few more slap-up-side-the-head moments, I can tell you. Time to take a good hard look at what I thought I was projecting as opposed to what everyone else was seeing. I decided to start with work. One of the main reasons people come to me in business as an interview coach is to find out what they are doing wrong. More often than not, what each of us is doing is not wrong but misinterpreted. What the other person or people see or hear when you speak or by what you do, is not matching with your intent.

I asked myself, "Is it something that needs to match?" The answer, in some ways... yes.

If they match, you/I are representing ourselves consistently. People out there in the big wide world are getting the right messages, the messages you want them to receive. Now achieving that consistency 100% of the time is pretty much impossible, you would have to be self-monitoring 24/7, so my aim is to try each day to be as consistent as I can and if I mess up, to own it. There is usually time to make amends or explain. I want the world to see the real me. Not the one built on past indiscretions and mistakes, not the one before I broke the mould perpetrated by my parents' beliefs or the poor decisions I made around friends or partners. **I want them to see the me that I have decided to be.**

Perception is something that can be checked quite easily, after all mixed messages will have consequences.

## BUT HOW DO YOU CHECK THAT? AHHHH I WAS HOPING YOU'D ASK… UP FOR IT?

Take a deep breath, this next exercise will test your open-mindedness.

**STAND UP
IF THE
'REAL YOU'
IS BEING SEEN?**

Anyone standing?

There is a distinct possibility that nobody is, you know why? At some stage in our lives most of us have thought, "people don't understand me", or "they cannot see what I have to offer" or "why can't they see who I really am?"

Figuring out what people are seeing or indeed what they think of you is confronting. I won't tip toe around that because it is. It is uncomfortable, it is exposing and most of us would rather be anywhere else than listening to what they, the world, have to say about us.

I put it to you that it is worth a little discomfort to find out. But you don't want open slather either; a few controls might be a good idea, or as I call them, strategies. One of my favourite strategies is encapsulated in this analogy: The 'First Date Scenario'. Hundreds if not thousands of my clients have heard this before:

*Interviews are like first dates, if you are blatantly honest and volunteer the good, the bad and the ugly, even if the other party asks, then it is highly unlikely that they will want to see you gain.*

The strategy I am advocating is one so that they, whoever they are, are not confused by the mixed messages of our often complex lives, but one that lets them see the real you. **You—at your very best.**

Understanding how others perceive you is a great asset in this quest. Take a deep breath and give this exercise a go.

**Step One**—Select four people, from different areas of your life (work, school, sport, family, community etc.)

**Step Two**—Tell them you are performing a 'Perception Edit' and would like them to fill in a form and answer some questions about you (Questions outlined on the next page). Explain to them that you want to find out how you are being perceived and if there is anything you might like to change in the way you are communicating.

Tell them it is to help you reach your goal of being seen for your authentic self. This is important, talk to them about being:

A) Constructive in their comments (no venting) and

B) Honest.

*Negative feedback that is not constructive is not welcome. This exercise is going to help highlight whether others are perceiving you in a similar way or an inconsistent way.*

**Step Three**—Gather the results, highlight any consistent responses on both the negative and positive side. Our objective is to identify and reinforce the positives, maybe even find out a few you had not realised but also to identify negative messages that more than one person is experiencing. Therefore providing you with the opportunity to change them, should you wish to.

## SUPER IMPORTANT NOTE

**Nothing your participants say necessarily means they are right.** It simply means that something in the way that you are communicating is sending a similar message to more than one person.

If you disagree with some of the feedback that's ok too. You may want to ask yourself is that negative response simply based on my relationship with that individual and that individual's needs, rather than something I need/want to change?

Have you got that form ready? It is often easier to fill in a form than to just write thoughts randomly.

The questions might look something like this:

**What am I really good at?**
*(List 4 specific but different areas.)*

**What are my best attributes/habits?**
*(List 4 specific but different areas.)*

**What could I be better at?**
*(List 4 specific but different areas.)*

**What are my negative attributes/habits?**
*(List 4 specific but different areas.)*

As I mentioned, this takes a little courage, from all parties.

The positive side will serve to reinforce those things that you project really well. You may even discover an attribute or skill you can add to that ever-growing list of 'stuff' you have to offer.

The negative side will be a teacher. Serving to highlight areas you might want to manage differently or that could be inadvertently holding you back.

This exercise **is not a free-for-all** for your nearest and dearest to say things they have always wanted to say. If their feedback is not constructive then that is their agenda, throw it out!!!

There was in fact one time that might serve to illustrate part of this exercise well. A time when I experienced an unexpected teaching moment. I was giving a speech at Sydney University with my wonderful friend Sue, CEO of The Pharmaceutical Locum Company.

We were in the auditorium presenting to a graduating Pharmacy class on careers. They, the soon to be Pharmacists, peered down at us from on high, the lecture room was like something out of an American university movie. The seating fanned out and upwards in a semi circular design, ascending until the back rows were a blur in the distance. Teacher and student were strategically disconnected by heavily stained dark wooden barricades. We, the speakers, a mere blob on the stage below. I always think it is around the wrong way—shouldn't we be on high, on stage like a concert, wonder what the reasoning behind this set up is?

It always takes me a bit to warm up, my voice a bit quivery when I begin. Nerves, we all have them, but once I get going I am on fire, at least that's how I perceive myself. We smashed it out and left the venue. We made our way to the car park, feeling rather chuffed with ourselves. "Tag-teamed the heck outta that presentation," I said. We laughed and carried on walking, each of us riding high on the adrenalin of the event.

Once in the car, Sue said, "Do you mind if I point something out?" "Ummmm, OK," I said, feeling a tiny bit confronted already. What was she going to say, did I mess up? This was her gig, I was just the ring in.

"Well," she said.

"You say 'OK' a lot when you are presenting."

"Do I?"

"Yep," she said, "It's not really necessary."

"OK," I said, tee he he...

After that first flush of 'I'm about to be criticized' left me, it was only seconds, I responded.

"I do, don't I? You know what, I think that is a habit I have formed as a coach. At regular intervals I would use 'OK' to check in to see if my client has understood our discussion. Especially the quiet ones. I think it gives me permission to move to the next point."

"Ah," she said, "I can see how that might be the case."

"You are right," I said. "I don't need to do that when presenting. I'll be more conscious of that next time around, thanks for making me aware of it."

Just like any one of us, the feeling that I had messed up or was about to be criticized was confronting. My natural instinct was to feel a little defensive. Instead of reacting I took the time for that initial feeling to pass (just a few seconds as I mentioned), realised it was said with love and respect and ended up taking the conversation as an opportunity to improve. Even negative feedback is an opportunity, it is all in the way we as individuals choose to react to it. Takes some work, but I now see it as my greatest asset. When my colleagues offer feedback about me, I listen, I try not to interrupt, I don't justify or leap to my own defence, I just listen. After which I decide if it is something I need to address or if I am OK (laughing) with it, just as it is.

I can't tell everyone else to question everything if I am not prepared to talk the talk and walk the walk.

SOME COMMUNICATION
HABITS MAY BE AFFECTING
HOW YOU ARE BEING
PERCEIVED.

HOW ARE YOU GOING TO CHANGE
OR MANAGE THE NEGATIVE FEEDBACK
FROM THIS EXERCISE?

*Note: An Interview Coach, Life Coach
or NLP Coach can help provide tools to manage
those areas you decide you would
like to change.*

## THE BIG QUESTION—WHAT DO EMPLOYERS WANT?

**If technical ability, experience or qualifications were all that mattered, people would be hired directly from their Resumé.**

But they are not.

## Why?

What do employers want? It's a tough question as let's face it, an employer's wants and needs differ depending on the industry as well as the position they wish to fill. But I can tell you that it is not just about experience and qualifications. About 50% of your hire-ability will be based on your 'fit' with the company, the team and its values. You might have heard this referred to as 'cultural fit'.

Sounds a bit like fluffy speak I know, but it might place people on a little more of an even playing field, whereas relying solely on qualifications and experience may not. If you think I see it as a good thing, you are correct. I prefer a well-rounded approach to recruitment that considers each person as a whole.

To put that in real terms, I'll start by illustrating what I look for when I try to find the right person to work in my team. We coach a vast range of people but our objective is one simple thing: **to help candidates prepare for job interviews by communicating effectively.**

Many major companies have HR consultants who specifically outline those soft skills or 'capabilities'. Yes, it is that important. Employers want to find the right fit as it a key indicator to how each employee feels valued, happy and to how long they may stay. A capability study is often used to define that fit clearly.

So here goes, my hiring capabilities, outside the qualification and experience requirements.

## My Capability Framework

**Do you really like what we do?** Caring about the type of work we do is crucial. We are helping people achieve their goals, our interaction is often very personal. You must have researched the company and be able to articulate what it is we do and why we do it. Irrespective of which position you are applying for.

**Be a thinker.** Most day-to-day stuff can be taught, so over and above that you will need an open mind. Open-minded people see opportunities and offer ideas, often they see things that I cannot. You like to think things through, take the blinkers off and see how things in business interconnect. Then act on that.

**You are a self-manager.** As a business owner I am not a hand-holder. I like to give you the reigns and let you run, no micro-managing here. That doesn't mean you can't have a bad day or be in need of support. It does mean you have to either manage it yourself or communicate whatever it is so we/I can help you.

**Show a willingness to step up.** "I can do that" is a phrase I love. If you want to give something a go, you can. The more you want to take on, the better, and you will be rewarded, I insist.

**Know what motivates you.** The biggest motivation we need is "I like to help people." Whether you are a Coach, IT, Admin, Social Media or Accounts, we are here to help each other and our candidates. Is that you?

**A solid level of self-knowledge.** None of us are perfect but knowing your weaknesses is just as important as your strengths. I will probably ask you about both.

A recent Pinstripe (my business) team member is an absolute gem, she pretty much has all of the above. When she started she said, "Kirst, I can handle all of those areas, but I'm not the face-to-face client person, I love being behind the scenes." Well, she knows herself, I thought. She has over-delivered on everything she has touched in a role that suits her capabilities.

> *"Everybody is a genius. But if you judge a fish by its ability to climb a tree, it will live its whole life believing that it is stupid."*
> Albert Einstein

## WHAT ARE THE CORE CULTURAL VALUES OF A COMPANY YOU WOULD WISH TO WORK FOR?

*Maybe that is how every job search should start.*

CHAPTER

6

# Ready to Finish Your Story?

*"You are the sum total of everything you've ever seen, heard, eaten, smelled, been told, forgot—it's all there. Everything influences each of us, and because of that I try to make sure that my experiences are positive."*

Maya Angelou

## HERE'S WHAT WE'VE GOT SO FAR

You've thought about what motivates you and stopped comparing yourself to anyone else.

Looked at relationships across every aspect of life and those you need to reassess.

Decided on a mentor, or a few.

Filled in an online dating profile just for laughs or a personality profile.

Read a few helpful hacks on being real, ego and getting on with it.

Fallen head over heels for failure, tenacity and resilience.

Listed the 'stuff' you inherently have.

You know you have to act in order to change anything.

You've grabbed your personal domain name and started creating some consistency across your social media.

Read inspiring stories about doing things differently.

Researched the company cultures that appeal to you.

Re-thought what defines you and it's not just your job.

Re-programmed self-beliefs and got a handle on perception.

Ditched a few communication habits you no longer needed.

Found out what employers want and which business cultural values appeal to you.

So what now?

What does all this tell me about me and my story? Or is that you and your story? Not to worry, I've ditched perfectionism and you get what I mean.

Either way, at this point you have now performed what I call 'The Gathering Phase'. You've compiled all this information about yourself, but it's rangy and disconnected, it needs to be compressed into your story in a more succinct manner.

Remember the 'Elevator Pitch'? The thinking here was that you need to be able to articulate your purpose, your goal, your business concept, whatever it is, in the time it takes to ride an elevator. That's not long. If you can't, then your message, your story, is too complex and the ability to grab the attention of the listener will be lost. The listener could be an employer, a partner, a project, a sports team, a client, in fact anyone. We don't call it that anymore, however the reason behind it remains the same. I call it 'this is me'.

While every scrap of this gathering phase is important and it is part of who you are today, at this point in time communicating that to others is the next challenge, one many of us struggle with.

Your story will of course continue to change, that's a given. So yes, you will have to revisit some of your decisions from time to time and each time you use your 'this is me' story, it may change. That's OK.

In the pursuit of pulling together the 'story of you' we must find the words that best describe all of those various parts of you, and that is our next line of thought.

On the following page I've added a list of career attributes. It's just a 'get started' list, select a few that define you at this point and you can add as many as you like, no limit.

## 'THIS IS ME' / CAREER-BRAND ATTRIBUTES

**Here are a list of ideas. Write down any that represent you at work, or add some new ones as they come to you.**

- Independent thinker
- Creative
- Takes direction well
- Fashion and trend conscious
- Not afraid to stand out
- Able to moderate communication style to suit a situation
- Likes to prepare in advance
- Can fly by the seat of your pants in areas of experience
- Connects with others on multiple levels
- Builds rapport easily
- Can hold your own no matter how much more experienced or educated a person is

- Hard working
- Reliable
- Empathetic
- Training ability
- Attempts new things
- Works well to time lines and budgets
- Researches
- Analyses
- Is motivated by others
- Is self-motivated
- Focused on further education
- Hands-on ability
- Ego mature
- Technically competent
- Big-picture thinker
- Sees areas for innovation or improvement
- Highly organised and systematic
- Project and planning ability
- Thrives on acts of service

## WHAT ATTRIBUTES HAVE YOU SELECTED?

4-5 would be good. It is difficult to remember more than that.

But it doesn't end there...

**Beside each point, add some quantified evidence from your experience that illustrates that attribute or strength.**

You will end up with two powerful things:

1. A summary of your career 'this is me' story.

2. The evidence to support that summary.

It might look something like this:

### Part 1—Attribute: Socially Adept

I relate to people on a variety of levels, that means whatever their experience I find a connection by asking questions and finding commonalities. In succinct terms it might be called socially adept.

### Part Two—Quantified Evidence

This has enabled me to grow the business by retaining customers to build a worldwide reputation. From a general part-time coach to specialising in aviation and coaching for 40+ airlines worldwide as well as training a specialist team of five coaches.

Irrespective of what role or project I will tackle next, that will still be my greatest ability or skill and a big part of my story.

As you can see there are two parts to the above statements. The first, describing my skill, strength or attribute and the second providing that 'quantified evidence'. Once you have 4-5 of these statements it is possible to condense them to form an impactful and authentic 'this is me' story.

When I completed this exercise for myself and my business I came up with these top 4 attribute phrases:

1. My focus is on being caring and supportive and unique.
2. Being accessible worldwide is crucial so we are 100% online.
3. My strength is being a socially adept communicator.
4. I only work with a network of senior experienced experts.

So what did it look like, my 'this is me' story, once condensed?

*I am a specialist aviation careers communication coach. I work globally via Skype. Our network of partners and coaches provides up-to-date impartial guidance for job seekers and we are here to support you every step of the way.*

And that...is how you do it.

## BECOME AN INFLUENCER

Part of building your story might be to create a following or a platform to project your unique voice out into the world. It's one way that you can create credibility around your profile, story or current career. Having a platform is a step towards becoming an Influencer. As an Influencer you have a fan base you know already likes what you are doing, one where you can build that new project you've had bubbling away in the back of your mind and present it to an existing audience.

**Why would you want to become an Influencer?** I suppose because an Influencer holds a little bit of power, power to introduce ideas and trends or to launch a brand, power to direct funds to good causes. **Influencers are conduits for change.**

The key word is power. With power you can advance issues or ideas that matter to you. Influencers sadly do not always use that power for good, we have seen them wield power in a negative or hurtful way to society. So whilst there will always be bullies using their power to intimidate, or high profile popular people who will misuse or misrepresent, each one of us has the ability to choose what type of influencer we want to be.

**Please choose wisely.**

# BLOGGING OR VIDEO BLOGGING (VLOGGING)

A fun way to start your Influencer quest is as a Blogger or Vlogger. Both can establish a person as an expert or thought leader in any area whatsoever. The trend is towards video as it is easier to consume, however the art of writing will never disappear. Content doesn't just have to be work-related. If you have ideas, perhaps around human interest, domestic or world issues, humour, fashion, you name it, you can build a following by 'ogging'. The other advantage is the little or zero amount of set up cost involved. Using existing social media outlets to promote your content such as Facebook and LinkedIn are vehicles that require very little outlay or risk.

Being a fairly good writer or speaker is a positive, but you know the audience you want to address, because you are probably part of it. More importantly it is your ability to relate to that audience, industry or fan base by using the type of language that suits your genre. That is the way to go. Your voice in text or audio is unique, so be you—everyone else is taken.

Someone said recently, "I've heard everyone has one book in them." Yes I've heard that too. Then she asked me, "How did you decide what to write about?" Great question! Took me a moment to respond. This book, I realised, was devised on the back of my blog. I saw what people related to and wanted to read as well as those blogs that fell flat so I decided to expand the popular blogs into this book. That process of deciding what to write about probably differs for everyone but if you want a starting place try this. **What do you wish someone had told you when you were younger?** Blog about that.

I blog about personal and work ideas, but my theme is consistent no matter the topic: 'Living your best life' and supporting others to do the same.

My topics range from:

- Personal Development
- TV Shows and World Issues
- Interviews
- Confidence
- Relationships
- Writing
- Social and Women's Issues
- Shoes (I love shoes) and of course Dogs

And the list goes on. If it matters to you, I say write about it, it probably matters to others too.

If you read Blogs or listen to Vlogs you'll notice there is a plethora of variety, nothing is off limits. The greatest motivation for some is to be as controversial as they can, straddling either side of the fence or issue dependent upon what creates the greatest response. If that is not your nature, that does not have to be the tack you take.

Personally I like to be thought-provoking rather than controversial. Blogging is a medium that creates relationships and relationships are built on being real.

- Real People
- Real Comments
- Real Observations

Remember my avoidance of over-produced perfection. That said, always have someone else proof your copy, it is next to impossible to proof your own work, as often you read what you thought you wrote, not what is actually on the page. For we dreadful spellers, even more pertinent.

**A word of warning**

Take custody of your ogging!

Once it is out, it is out.

Try having a yard stick for self-censoring.

One that aligns with your values.

"Would I be happy to say this to my Grandmother?"

or

"Am I prepared to navigate negative discourse or criticism on this topic?"

**Use it as a force for good.**

**Use it as a force for change.**

**Use it as a force for creativity.**

**Use it to be a disrupter.**

Your Blog/Vlog will after all form part of your legacy.

## DECIDING WHAT TO BLOG/VLOG ABOUT?

**Think back to the social media posts where you felt compelled to comment or to share as you were deciding your 'I'm Into' list.**

When you share a post or comment, it is often for one of these reasons:

- It is a topic that compels you to act.
- It is humorous.
- It provokes a feeling you relate to.

**Why not 'og' on one of those?**

## FINDING THE DISRUPTER IN YOU

Don't Do What Everyone Else Is Doing

Finding those Blog topics may well set you on a path to defining where you want to make your mark or make a difference. While most things have been done before or regurgitated in random forms, taking another run at them from your perspective is not a bad thing. If you wait until you have a fully-fledged, thoroughly worked up, awesomely unique idea you could be waiting forever.

Why not take an existing idea and turn it on its head? That is what a Disrupter does.

I'll use fashion as a showcase for this re-working principle. You will have noticed that trends from the 80s came back in the 2000s but with a twist. Flares have come and gone a few times, as has animal print anything and my favourite, the super high-waisted pant. *Really?* No. Who the heck can rock those things?

The twist is what matters. Even though double denim was done to double death in the 80s it was revived, reinvented, restyled and repackaged for a new audience in 2017. Every year it will be something else, repackaged. The fun thing about repackaging existing ideas is that your audience is always changing. While those humbugs from the 80s are spouting, "We did that back then," it's going to be super fresh to anyone who came after that.

If we listen to Amanda Priestly from 'The Devil Wears Prada', it was fashion editors around the world who decided what all of us would be wearing each season. But did the Amandas of the world really reinvent the new season's looks or did they just jump on the bandwagon of a fashion influencer and use their prowess as media moguls to spread the trend?

I think it could have happened either way.

A Disrupter says to themselves, "I don't give a rat's patootee how it has always been done, I'm doing it my way." There are no guarantees whatsoever that it will work. It is a risk, sure, but what if it does, what if everyone jumps on board, what if it takes off? You will never know until you try.

Disruption starts when you decide to take a look at how you do things day-to-day and ask the question; **"Is there a better way?"**

This is how asking that very question went for me a couple of years back.

I started by coaching clients in person, just the two of us, one-on-one. They would travel to see me from New Zealand, all over Australia, Papua New Guinea, Asia and the Middle East, adding a huge cost to them, not only in travel but in time away from work and sometimes accommodation. They liked it that way. I cannot tell you how many times I would say, "We can work together over SKYPE or Facetime," and heard "No, I'd rather come in and see you face-to-face, online won't be as good." My reply to their push back was, "OK, that's what my clients want." I had sort of resigned myself to it. The problem was I was busy—too busy. Seeing people in person added about 20-30 minutes of unpaid meet, greet and chat time to my schedule. Something had to change but my clients refused to buy into it, or seemed to. Eventually I gave up and for too many years I felt I was stuck with the face-to-face model.

Then that day came, I had had enough, either this coaching gig changes or I throw in the towel from pure exhaustion. I wasn't so much angry, just disappointed in myself for not taking the reins earlier and getting to this frazzled state. It was that point, the one of no return, that severely reduced the perceived risk factor. The risk of losing my clients was holding me in a state of safety rather than one of change and growth.

## Change or fold. The time was now.

Just because this is how coaches have always worked does not mean it has to stay this way.

After the hissy fit subsided another thought popped into my head. What if they are just wrong? What if online coaching is just as good and they are simply not willing to change their belief that coaching online was less personal or not as effective? What if I take away their choice, online or nothing? What would they do? Mild panic at that thought, but resolve not defeated.

Look at the benefits to my business, I could coach anywhere in the world at any time. I could take on other coaches who could also have the flexibility to work from home. We could decentralise our processes via the cloud or an online database. As for the big picture, if I had to rely on the limitations of my time hour-by-hour I simply could not grow the business or create the lifestyle that I craved.

The benefits were obvious. They outweighed the risk of failure so I champed firmly down on the bit and did it. Not a little at a time mind you, 100% in. Just like my friend Rob Brus at "Go All In" podcast says: *"When you go all in you give your best to the world. You are making it a better place, you are living up to your true potential."*

Here goes. Step 1: Automate. Step 2: Find authentic new coaches who were up for it. Step 3: Announce that all coaching would now be performed online without exception. Step 4: Expand, expand, expand.

Of course I was worried. This was my baby, my sole income and my reputation. Would my clients go for it? Would I lose some who felt they were not getting value? Would they accept other coaches? Would having to use technology put them off? I am not afraid to admit that these concerns kept me up at night. They were all valid, and in an industry based around personal interaction the risk was high. Also, nobody else was doing it in this way within my niche. Was there a reason for that? The great unknown reared its ugly head and a feeling of anguish was with me constantly.

And there it was, the push back came quickly. Some long-term clients insisted they needed to fly in to see me. OK, this is a transition period, I told myself. We ran an intensive campaign to promote the benefits and convenience of our new coaching program as well as a re-education program before cutting them off totally (nicely, of course).

Ultimately within a couple of months all new clients went onto the online model with little or no fuss. The relief was palpable. While my broader vision was about working differently and lifestyle (namely having one), it was also top of mind that any disruption to the way things were traditionally done still had to benefit our customers. It had to work for both of us. I am pleased to say that we were able to reach far more people and automating our systems actually provided a platform that enabled us to streamline the entire way the business ran. I too was no longer getting to the point of burn-out. In today's world that might not seem like such a big bold idea, however in my industry it certainly was. I had learnt to back myself, think more strategically and plan for some fall out—and there is always fall out.

Shortly after the re-launch someone commented that they loved my business model and called me a Disrupter. I then looked it up. Arnie Bellini, CEO of ConnectWise describes it this way: *"Simply put, a disrupter is someone who isn't afraid to make waves, someone who is constantly pushing the envelope to do things better, without worrying about how things have always been done."*

**Here It Is—The Fallout.** Speaking of fall out, it is real. I am going to assume you have experienced it even in some small way, be it on Facebook when you posted YES or NO in the same sex marriage debate or Brexit or having alternate views on climate change.

We had four months of 50% revenue drop. I had to refund some long-term clients who cancelled appointments and although I had planned for the downturn, it took longer than projected. Being a Disrupter has both positive and negative fallout. Not all as immediate as on social media, but there will be some. Your strategy will help to counter it. Measuring and understanding the responses is essential. If the fallout is from a faction that matters most to you, maybe you need to re-enact the re-education phase of your strategy. Don't throw it away the minute the negatives roll in. Disrupting and influencing takes time, it takes message consistency along with education and exposure. Change is slow and steady and requires reassurance.

**Hold your ground.**

**Commit to your vision.**

The next time you hear:

"That's the way we have always done things"

Take that as a challenge.

WHAT NEEDS TO CHANGE?
(IN YOUR WORK
& PERSONAL LIFE)

IS THERE IS A BETTER WAY?

AM I READY TO TAKE IT ON?

CHAPTER

7

# I'm Not in Sales or Marketing

## WHAT'S IN A TITLE?

YOUR TITLE OR EXPERIENCE MAY NOT include the words 'Sales' or 'Marketing'. I get that. The fact that those particular words are missing means nothing at all. I put it to you that all of us must be our very own sales, marketing and promotions team in order to achieve anything we set out to achieve. Simple as that.

Whether your career is in finance, teaching, construction, aviation, emergency services, tourism or you are a tradesperson. Whether you are a musician, a school student, charity volunteer, writer or a mum on the teacher/parent committee you are in fact in sales and marketing in some way.

We are constantly told in business that "business is about sales." It is irrelevant what your business is about or what role you have within it. Whomever you come into contact with, you are creating an experience, one they will either remember or forget. That's exactly what selling and marketing are.

I am suggesting that this does not apply solely to business. Whatever your chosen career or position in life, you are in the business of promotion, self-promotion that is.

If you desire to progress in that career or achieve personal or family goals you must advocate for them. Therefore you must be heard. Being heard requires making a noise; making noise means you have a point to get across and people who need to listen... your market.

So, you are in marketing—welcome.

Next thought: if everyone is in marketing, what if you don't know what you are marketing? Good question, I am about to discuss that further.

## WHAT IS MARKETING?

Here are few of my favourite definitions:

*"Marketing is creating irresistible experiences that connect with people personally and create the desire to share with others."*
Saul Colt, Head of Magic, Fresh Books

*"Marketing is the act of developing an engaging relationship with every single human being that shows an interest in you."*
Paul Flanigan, Consultant, Experiate.net

*"Marketing is anything you create or share that tells your story."*
Ann Handley, Chief Content Officer, MarketingProfs,
Author with C.C. Chapman of *Content Rules*

*"Marketing is the art and science of persuasive communication."*
Dave Kerpen, Chief Executive Officer, Likeable Media

## WHAT DO YOU HAVE THAT THE MARKET WANTS?

Remember you are not necessarily marketing a product or service. You may be marketing you and your potential. If you don't know what you have that is worth marketing, it's time to find out. Because if you don't know, then how is anyone else going to?

You need to decide.

PS: (whiny little inside head voice) I don't care if you think you have nothing special and are no different to everyone else going for this job or creating this project, **you are wrong—reality check!**

## THERE IS NOBODY JUST LIKE YOU. NOBODY WHO HAS YOUR EXACT EXPERIENCES OR APTITUDES ANYWHERE ELSE IN THE WORLD

As for marketing, it is about connection.

When you connect with someone you are **building rapport**, rapport in its purest form is making someone feel something.

When you **invoke feelings** you have found something that matters to someone.

Apply everything you have questioned so far in *The Albino Chameleon*. Take those decisions and use them as tools that help to define you, that provide clarity and the language to articulate you and your story. The answers to those questions have bought us to this point, one where you have the ability and insight to illustrate what you have to offer and your unique story.

WHEN WAS THE LAST TIME
YOU MADE SOMEONE FEEL
SOMETHING, ANYTHING?

WHAT WAS THE TOPIC
OF CONVERSATION?

*Be it a connection or caring, confusion or concern, positive or negative, they paid attention to what you did or said.*

*When you see how your story connects with people then those people, well, they are your market.*

# CHAPTER 8

# Chameleon Take-Aways

*Your story is a unique one.*

*Your experiences belong only to you.*

*You are an individual in every way.*

*That in itself is valuable.*

The more people I meet, the more I realise how interesting people are and also how much each person has that I can learn from.

Become a sponge; soak up your 'people experiences'.

Investing time in others is ultimately investing in yourself.

During this adventure, if you have realised or decided just one thing about yourself, one thing that you can articulate, then this project has been worthwhile.

If you have in turn acted upon something, I shall consider it a complete success.

# ALBINO CHAMELEON COMMANDMENTS

*No comparisons.*

*Break the rules.*

*Stop thinking and act.*

*Take custody of your words.*

*Show up.*

*Everyone remembers things differently.*

*Acknowledge the input of others.*

*Tell people you love them.*

*Stop waiting.*

*Take calculated risks.*

*Work on your health, without it life is less.*

*Be vulnerable.*

*Work smarter not harder.*

*Do something you believe in.*

*Ask for what you want.*

*Be ruthless with your standards.*

*Surround yourself with people you aspire to.*

*Agree to disagree.*

*Think of your life as a book and give it a title.*

*Don't be reactive.*

*People come first, full stop.*

*Celebrate your inner weirdo.*

*Animals equal unconditional love.*

*Stand up for yourself and others.*

*Accept differences.*

*Laugh a lot, including at yourself.*

*Give without expecting anything.*

*Listen.*

Everyone has a story, it is my hope you will build your story and that it will help to enact your goals and ultimately form part of your legacy, after all...

The craziest thing you will ever do is nothing.

# From Ben

For most of my life I saw my major difference as a disadvantage, a hurdle. Being an Albino Chameleon was something that got in the way of well, everything. As I grew to understand myself I saw that my fellow chameleons were just as unique, it was not as obvious at first glance, I had to dig a little deeper. I had to take the time to get to know each one in order to see how special each chameleon was and how interesting.

I also learnt that the things that make us wonderful and grant us the opportunity to do something worthwhile in life were held in those very unique aspects of each of us. My difference was heralded to all by my lack of the beautiful colours that symbolise belonging to a tribe, the tribe of chameleon. But in reality what made me unique was who I decided to be on the inside.

Pardalis became known to other chameleon communities as the place that you can find acceptance and I'm OK with that, what a wonderful legacy to leave behind.

# A Gift From Ben to You

For a Summary of all the questions used to develop your story, unmask your super power and discover the many shades of your chameleon, with space to write your notes, ideas and actions...

**Head to:**

**www.kirstyanneferguson.com**

And download your gift.

# Glossary of Strange Terms

Life Armoury—*The defence techniques we build over time to save us from pain or hurt.*

Gate Keepers—*A person or persons who are attempting to keep you from something, somewhere or someone.*

Give It A Crack—*Australian slang for give it a go.*

Ring-In—*Someone who has come into the conversation or event who was originally not invited or included.*

Muppet—*A person who is generally ignorant, has no idea about anything but can laugh at themselves.*

Tad—*Just a little bit.*

Rat's Patootee—*I don't care, or I don't give a damn. Used in place of the "F" word.*

Disrupter—*Someone obsessed with change and doing things differently. An innovator or ideas person challenging industry norms.*

Influencer—*Social media term for a person with a large following who can promote brands or ideas to their platform.*

Hissy Fit—*An uncontrollable fit brought about by a person in a bad mood who is taking it out on others.*

Shemozzle—*A total mess. Me most Fridays.*

Airy Fairy—*Impractical, emotional or idealistic.*

Random—*Used as a modern cultural reference for anything out of place or unexpected.*

Ego Maturity—*Self-confidence while maintaining a humble 'nice person' status.*

# About the Author

Kirsty is a New Zealander who has spent much of her adult life in Australia. Following infertility, a failed marriage, the deaths of both parents and younger brother, she decided that the next half of her life would be dedicated to opportunity and optimism.

Kirsty reinvented her fledging coaching business as a global online brand specialising in aviation careers. Her team of off site coaches works in 20 countries across 45 airlines. She has been referred to a 'personal publicist' a 'confidence cheer-squad' and the 'oracle of interviews'. Her clients often call her the 'O…. of Interviews (referring to a certain megastar talk show host who we won't name).

She uses her platform to advocate for women in minority roles, for school leavers and career changers. Posting as a thought leader, blogger and mentor, encouraging self-knowledge, change and innovation across any field.

Kirsty has lectured at Sydney and Griffith Universities. You can read her monthly columns in *Australian Aviation* Magazine,

World of Aviation and online at www.aviationjobsearch.com. She has been interviewed for: Reuters, News.com.au, *Marie Claire* magazine and *Coaching Life*. You can listen to her interviews as a guest and presenter on Apple Podcast **'Go All In'** and **Australian Aviation Radio**.

# Author Profile

www.kirstyanneferguson.com
www.thealbinochameleon.com

**Business Profile**
www.pinstripesolutions.com

**Linkedin**
www.linkedin.com/in/kirstyfergusonpinstripe/

**Contributing Author**
*Australian Aviation* magazine
*World of Aviation* magazine
www.australianaviation.com.au
www.aviationjobsearch.com

**Blog**
www.pinstripesolutions.com/blog/
www.linkedin.com/in/kirstyfergusonpinstripe/
detail/recent-activity/posts/

**Instagram**
'The Albino Chameleon Speaks'
www.instagram.com/kirstyanneferguson
@kirstyanneferguson
#thealbinochameleon
#kirstyanneferguson
#pinstripesolutions

www.ingramcontent.com/pod-product-compliance
Ingram Content Group UK Ltd.
Pitfield, Milton Keynes, MK11 3LW, UK
UKHW041410180426
11947UKWH00007B/49